STAND UP!

Resilient Black Women Who Are Shaping the World With Their Faith

D1286546

ArDenay Garner

ISBN-13: 978-1-954609-20-4

Library of Congress Control Number: 2021925066

For information regarding special discounts for bulk purchases, please contact the publisher:
LaBoo Publishing Enterprise, LLC
staff@laboopublishing.com
www.laboopublishing.com

Scripture quotations marked (NLT) are taken from the Holy Bible, New Living Translation, copyright ©1996, 2004, 2015 by Tyndale House Foundation. Used by permission of Tyndale House Publishers, Inc., Carol Stream, Illinois 60188. All rights reserved.

Scripture quotations marked (NIV) are taken from the Holy Bible, New International Version®, NIV®. Copyright © 1973, 1978, 1984, 2011 by Biblica, Inc.™ Used by permission of Zondervan. All rights reserved worldwide. www.zondervan.com

The Holy Bible, King James Version. Cambridge Edition: 1769; *King James Bible Online*, 2019. www.kingjamesbibleonline.org.

Scripture quotations marked ESV are from the Holy Bible, English Standard Version, copyright © 2001 by Crossway Bibles, a publishing ministry of Good News Publishers. Used by permission. All rights reserved.

The Living Bible copyright © 1971 by Tyndale House Foundation. Used by permission of Tyndale House Publishers Inc., Carol Stream, Illinois 60188. All rights reserved.

Scripture taken from the New King James Version®. Copyright © 1982 by Thomas Nelson. Used by permission. All rights reserved.

Scripture quotations marked TPT are from The Passion Translation®. Copyright © 2017, 2018 by Passion & Fire Ministries, Inc. Used by permission. All rights reserved. ThePassionTranslation.com.

Zondervan Publishing House. The Amplified Bible (1965). Thirtieth printing, March 1985. Library of Congress Catalog Card Number 65-19500.

CONTENTS

INTRODUCTION

If you knew what God really needed from you, would you say yes? If you knew that there was more that God required of you, would you say yes? If you knew everything that you were predestined to do before the world began, would you still say yes?

As the visionary author of STAND UP! I gave God an obedient yes to stand up and do His will. I said yes, without having the full vision or knowing the requirements to coordinate this collection. I can recall the exact moment when God spoke to me during my seven and a half mile walking meditation at Onondaga Lake Park. He asked me to pivot my coaching business to exclusively help women develop their purpose through writing their personal stories to promote compassion and world healing. I vividly remember telling God, "I am not a writing coach. There are thousands of writing coaches already; that's not what I do. I am a personal development coach." Go figure: I was telling God what I do, as if He did not already know. You see, that is the beauty of having a personal relationship with God. You can talk with Him as you would your best friend. In response to my clarification, God said, "I am not asking you to be a writing coach. I want you to support women in their transformation from ideation to publication in their pursuit of becoming a published author. You will support them as a personal development trainer. Your niche will be aspiring non-fiction authors."

After a decade of uncertainty, confusion, frustration, and experimentation in business, I received my marching orders from God. I was clear on my next steps and how to move forward. On June 12, 2021, God officially became the chief executive officer of my business and subsequently my life because I was finally in alignment with His will. My life's purpose and business mission were the same. God instructed me to allow Him and only Him to lead me. He said that He would be my coach, expert, guru, strategist, mentor, and leader and that I did not need to consult with anyone except Him for my business at this time. What a relief. After all these years I received a direct answer from God to the question "Who is your target audience?" It felt surreal. Heaven's gate opened and poured out an unexpected blessing shortly after I had been weeping and praying for direction and guidance. In an instant, my life was uncomplicated. Once again, I was hopeful and enthused about being an entrepreneur.

Before I could fully rejoice in the spirit, God said, "Let me be clear: This is not about you. This is about developing the human potential and bringing My people closer to Me." With that additional revelation, I knew God was expanding my ministry to serve, which now included a special population of aspiring non-fiction authors. I threw my hands up in the air, turned my head toward the sun rays beaming on the lake, smiled, and began to silently thank God. I assured Him I was clear on my new assignment and ready and willing to proceed in walk-on-water faith with total reliance on Him.

What you are about to experience in STAND UP! are the incredible stories of resilient Black women who said "YES" to doing God's will. Each contributing author agreed to share their personal story of forgiveness, reconciliation, survivorship, perseverance, obedience, love, and faith to support your healing and deliverance from people, places, and situations that are holding your mind hostage and preventing you from living out your destiny.

is strong; yea, a man of knowledge increaseth strength." So I stayed in the Word as much as possible. Even though I was growing closer to the Lord, I was still walking by sight and not by faith in some areas of my life. Wanting to regain my relationship with my son, the rejection of a non-responsive text or call was killing me. That hurt was deep, but his hurt was far deeper. I was an absent mother. I had to stop looking for responses and just stand in faith, with a surrendered heart.

Believing that God would remove some of the pain and hurt I caused him, I began to only send him text messages stating that I loved him and to have a great day. I stayed consistent with that for a long time. No expectations, only faith in God. I was so thankful that my daughter and I could have conversations every once in a while. She never took sides or judged me. I knew she loved both her parents, regardless. But I also knew this had to have an effect on her in some kind of way. No one escapes from the hand of divorce without some type of scars. My prayer has always been and will forever be, *Lord, cover and protect the minds of my children, help them to seek You first and Your righteousness in all that they do. Remind them that they are loved and that no man or woman can separate them from that love you have toward them. Bless them, Father God, in every area of their lives, for they are wonderful children and a blessing to us as parents and to the world. Continue to stretch them in the gifts and talents you placed inside them. Let them never be ashamed to share the gospel, the good news, to others. Strengthen them in the areas where they are weak and remind them that you are their help in a time of trouble. People, such as their mother, may fail them but you, oh Lord, NEVER FAIL OR FORSAKE US! So Father God, remove the deep scars that may be hidden in the hearts of my two children and replace them with the light of Jesus, the love of God, and the joy of the Holy Spirit. For my faith is the substance of things hoped for and the evidence of things not seen. God, there is nothing impossible with You.*

The year 2020 arrived and every prophet was speaking about God giving us 20/20 vision for the year, yet no one saw this pandemic coming! It set the ENTIRE world at a standstill. God was and is showing us that we are nothing without Him. We need Him every moment of each day He allows us to see. With all the calls and text messages, and the news reporting people passing, near and far, fear and anxiety clutched the nation, myself included. I began having the lonely feeling again, being at home and no one to converse with. I worked every day because my job never shut down due to the company being essential. Most of us were afraid and unsure about the safety of being too close to one another, so I always kept my distance as much as possible, knowing that God is my protector and my healer.

While on vacation for two weeks in the month of April 2020, my ex-husband reached out to me by phone. I was so elated to hear from him because he usually just sends text messages sporadically. But this time he called and we talked for about two hours. Oh my goodness, I enjoyed our conversation immensely. It felt as if I had company over—just what I needed to calm the anxiety. It was a delight to speak of positive things instead of the normal conversations everyone else was having about the dreaded COVID-19 virus. He was calling me quite often and I was thankful for it. We would talk for hours, mostly of our jobs, our children and grandson, and how good God is. While the months were going by, we both continued to keep in touch with each other when we had time, both of us working through the pandemic and trying to stay safe. The new year was approaching and I was preparing myself to move to Georgia, to be closer to my daughter and grandson. Realizing how short life can be, I really wanted to be near family and not feel so lonely anymore.

With half of my home packed up and ready to move, in April of 2021 I became extremely ill. I was having symptoms months prior, difficulty swallowing and digesting my food, chest pains/burning, anxiety and acid reflux. I took a visit to my primary doctor; she sent me to a Gastroenterologist, who in turn diagnosed me with H-Pylori (Helicobacter Pylori) which means bacterial infection in the gut. I was out from work for two months with this debilitating disease. Fear started to rear its head as I feared I could die alone and no one would know. My family and friends would text or call me to see how I was; this included my ex-husband, my son and daughter, but I really needed help. By this time, I was so frail and extremely weak. I ended up staying with my wonderful and caring sisters for three weeks.

As I started getting slightly better each day, in mid-July, I remember praying to God early in the morning about not wanting to be alone. About four hours after that prayer my ex-husband called me and said, "Hey, when we get settled in (he and my son), I'm going to call for you to come here and stay with us." I couldn't believe what I was hearing. My Lord. God is calling for us to reconcile. I told him that when the Lord tells him it's time for me to come, then call his wife home. Hallelujah! God can turn everything around for your good. From Fornication to Forgiveness to Faith to going back to my FAMILY.

Dedication

All Glory and Honor to my Lord Jesus Christ. Special thanks to ArDenay Garner for helping me to step out on faith in writing my first chapter for an anthology. I dedicate this to all the readers; may your lives be forever changed by the testimonies of all the resilient Black women who STOOD UP to the challenge. Blessings to my entire family and my friends, much love to you all. To God be the glory forever!

Karen Lawrence is a believer in Christ. She is a business owner and the President of IMA Events in Charlotte, NC. She volunteers for church activities, serving her local community. She and her husband, Ira, work alongside their son, Ira Dubb, Founder of Bunk 57 Ministries to mentor young men ages 12-17, and assists formally incarcerated citizens in returning home with dignity.

Karen's future plans are to implement a support group for women with incarcerated children.

MY EYES WILL SEE YOUR GLORY

Karen R. Lawrence

And I am sure that God who began the good work within you will keep right on helping you grow in his grace until his task within you is finally finished on that day when Jesus Christ returns. Philippians 1:6, TLB

I learned to cast all my cares on the Lord and to know that God can mend a broken heart, especially when it comes to our children. To be broken is to be forcibly separated into two or more pieces. There are many forms of brokenness, like the death of a loved one, a broken marriage, or a severed relationship. My brokenness came from the forcible separation of my child from us by the justice system. Trials in life come to make us stronger. God is not surprised by anything that happens in our journey of life. However, we learn through trials whether we can pass the test. My story is not about what many would consider a tragedy. It is about the heart of a mother and the love she has for her children. Nothing can break our hearts more than when things go wrong with our children. How do you stand in faith when the vision you have for your child does not go the way you think it should go? My story is also about forgiveness, redemption, and victory in God. From experience, I know that God will put the pieces of your life back together if you stand in prayer, faith, obedience and forgiveness. The combination of all these things allows us to grow stronger in Him.

We live in a world today where our children are under major attack by the enemy. Demons in the spiritual realm have been released with the assignment to destroy our young men and women at an early age, before they can ever have a chance to live a productive life as God has commanded. Our children are growing up angry and hating each other and themselves. The love of God is growing cold in their hearts. We live in a society where images of violence and selfishness are flooding our minds 24 hours a day. Our society celebrates, honors and awards bad behavior and foolishness. We have gotten away from simple respect and have lost the art of communication, to reason things out with conversation versus a bullet. Many of us parents have been lulled to sleep by Satan. We no longer stand watch and fight in faith for the very soul of our children.

The enemy has come in like a flood to make our black and brown children look at each other or themselves with so much hate, to the point that life is meaningless, making it easier to take their own life or another's without even a blink. Gone are the days of the good old fist fights. Gone are the days of community discipline and respect. I share my story with mothers who have had to fight in faith for your child's life and spirituality. I encourage you to fight with your spiritual weapons to defeat the schemes of the enemy and to cancel every assignment meant to destroy your child's life.

You are the source of my strength and the strength of my life...

From a child, I have always had faith. At times, it may not have been much, but it was there. That mustard seed faith has seen me through five decades. My early years as a child were with my grandparents in the South. My grandmother kept my brother and me active in church. We attended church services, Sunday School and Vacation Bible School. My grandmother was well known in the community, serving in the church, running the church daycare center and a chapter of the Boy Scouts. I fondly think of her each time I hear the song "His Eye is on the Sparrow" ...so I know He watches me, because that was one of her favorite songs to sing. She was a strict disciplinarian. At times I felt she was too harsh, but then, I was looking through the lens of a child. One fateful night, at the age of 12, my grandfather woke me up urging me to get help. He said, "Your grandmother is sick; call an ambulance." I made the call, but since we lived in a poor black neighborhood, there was no sense of urgency on their part. The one question they asked before they would dispatch an ambulance was, "Do you have $25 to pay for the service?" I looked at my grandfather and said, "Granddaddy, they are asking if we have $25?" "Tell them yes, please come," he said. I gave them our address. I don't know how long it took, but when they eventually got there, all they did was shine a flashlight in her face and pronounce her dead. I saw white faces that made no effort to revive her. Dead—my grandmother was gone. I watched her die in my grandfather's arms, holding her heart with white foam coming from her mouth. Dead of a heart attack. This was my first experience and struggle with faith. How did God let this happen?

As I grew into my teenage years, I enjoyed my life. I was raised in a single-parent household by my father. However, I was like any other teen. I participated in extracurricular activities at school, worked a part-time job and did things I knew I was not supposed to do. I tried experimenting with smoking cigarettes, marijuana, drinking, hanging out at games and parties and, of course, sex. I never tried anything hardcore, too afraid of that and always, in the back of my mind, was the discipline I would receive if I got caught.

I became pregnant at 19, before marriage. I had finished school so that wasn't a problem, but I was so afraid to tell my father and to see his disappointment in me. However, I was determined that I was going to be a good mother. The delivery of my son was difficult. My labor had to be induced because I suffered from toxemia. The baby was coming early. I remember the doctor telling me in the emergency room that I would need to deliver soon to keep them from losing me, my baby or both of us. The faith and prayers of my family and in-laws brought me through eighteen hours of labor and a week stay in the hospital because I was so sick.

When my son was about three years old, I had a dream. I dreamt that I was standing in the middle of a road between my son and a big black blob. I was trying to keep this blob from overtaking him and I was in a battle with this thing. Having one foot in the door of the church at the time, I never understood why I dreamt something like this but today, I understand. I believe God was letting me know that the enemy would try to overtake my son and that I was going to have to stand in the gap to keep this from happening. The prayers of the righteous would keep him from being consumed. Although I was raised going to church, as a teenager, I strayed. I did not take church seriously although I knew the Word. However, through a series of marital arguments (we were both so young) my husband and I decided that we wanted to make our marriage work, so it was time to get serious about what we both knew. We needed to spend time in the Word and dedicate our lives to Christ. As I matured in the Word, I began to confess that the fruit of my womb would be blessed. This was God's promise and I continue to stand on this scripture today. (Deuteronomy 28:4)

Battle for my son

These trials are only to test your faith, to see whether or not it is strong and pure. It is being tested as fire tests gold and purifies it— and your faith is far more precious to God than mere gold; so, if your faith remains strong after being tried in the test tube of fiery trials, it will bring you much praise and glory and honor on the day of his return. 1Peter 1:7, TLB

In November of 2014, a few days before Thanksgiving, my husband and I got a call in the middle of the night. It was my son calling from a police department in Georgia. "Ma, I just want to let you know that I have been arrested, but I am okay. I hit a man on a motorcycle." At those words, my heart dropped. "Is he dead?" I asked. "I don't know." What happened? "He was messing with me in traffic, so I hit him with the car. I will call you back when I get out of here." As a mother whose child was in trouble, I had an assortment of feelings: glad that my son was alive in this day and time, and angry that he would do something so crazy in my opinion. Hurt because I saw this messing up his life and ashamed that he had been arrested, especially when we raised him different. Fast forward a year later: We were in court. I knew I had to rely on faith to get us through. I went into the restroom at the courthouse to pray. I prayed for God to show us His mercy and bring about a miracle. I called on heaven and all its angels to surround my son, my husband and myself, that we would be protected and walk out as a family. Not having the best representation and being ill advised by his attorney, my son was sentenced to 20 years–five years in prison and a 15-year probation. The victim asked the judge to make an example of him and to give him life. As I watched my son being handcuffed and carried away immediately, all these angry and hurt feelings I had struggled with came roaring to the surface in full force.

My pain was great. This was my child. My heart was broken. My son was being snatched from us in a sense and there was nothing, I mean nothing, I could do about it. There would be years of not being able to see him succeed in his career, share birthdays or holidays, vacations or just doing the things we had always done together. A senseless act of aggression and I blamed him, I blamed myself, I blamed the "so-called" victim, I blamed the attorney, I blamed the system. How could life be so unfair? I wanted to retaliate against this man who started this altercation with my son and walked away with no discipline from our justice system.

Later that night after we drove four hours back home, he called us. "Ma, I am so sorry to disappoint you and Daddy. However, I told the truth and am owning up to what I did but the [victim] said several things that were an absolute lie. It is not over until God says it's over," he told us. "I am going to do what I must do to get through this and move on with my life." I told my son that we had a choice. We could either go through this dark valley with God or without. Which would it be? "With God," he said.

The Devil Condemns but God Redeems

Now the salvation and the power and the kingdom of our God and the authority of his Christ have come, for the accuser of our brothers has been thrown down, who accuses them day and night before our God. Revelation 12:10. *There is therefore now no condemnation for those who are in Christ Jesus.* Romans 8:1, KJV

The devil condemns but God redeems – God is going to write his story. For three months and through the first set of holidays, he was not allowed to call or write us, and we were not able to make contact with him. Those three months were hell for me, not knowing if he was okay or what was really going on. After going through the evaluation at the intake prison, he was able to make contact once he transferred to where he would serve his time. During his incarceration, I made sure that he called us every day. We just needed to hear his voice and for him to let us know that he was okay. There were times I was so hurt and so worried that I found myself in a fetal position on my bedroom floor with tears streaming from my eyes. Did I question God? Absolutely! What went wrong? Was I a good mother? Did I give wrong advice to my child? What could I have changed or done differently? Why did it even happen? I would hear other parents bragging about their children - about how well they were doing academically or finding success in their careers. Although I was truly happy for them, I was hurting on the inside.

Release my shame

Do not let me be put to shame, nor let my enemies triumph over me. No one who hopes is in you will ever be put to shame, but shame will come on those who are treacherous without cause. Show me your ways, Lord, teach me your paths. Guide me in your truth and teach me, for you are God my Savior, and my hope is in you all day long. Psalm 25:2, NIV

I felt ashamed. I was ashamed of my son; I was ashamed of myself. Not only that, but my heart was broken. How could this young man, who we raised to do the right thing, and who I had so many hopes and dreams for, get into this kind of trouble? Never in a million years did I think my son would serve time in prison. When people would ask, "How is your son doing?" I would say, "Oh, he's fine." "Is he coming home for the holidays?" "No, he won't be able to make it this time." On and on it went as I fought to keep a smile on my face. I was ashamed to tell people the truth. I did not want them to judge him or us as parents. More than that, why should I care? This was my child, and I would stand by him, regardless of other peoples' thoughts.

In church we would always laugh and say, "Tell the truth, shame the devil." When I began to share what happened to my son, it delivered me. So many women began to open up and share their stories about their own experiences, run-ins their children had with the justice system.

These women told stories of the pain, the stress, and the financial cost of their child being in trouble. They didn't judge me but let me know they had experienced the same feelings I had felt. I was not alone. However, I was saddened by the fact that so many women were keeping their pain silent, just like me. It hurts not being able to share but when you do share, a burden is lifted from your heart and soul.

Another dear friend of mine described it as people having a "secret heart." We all have one. There are some things in our lives that are too painful to talk about, so we keep it hidden and refuse to speak about it or share with anyone else. When we hold painful experiences in our secret hearts, the enemy gets the victory. We overcome the power of the enemy by the blood of the lamb and by word of our testimony. (Revelation 12:11)

You are the righteousness of God. (Romans 5:17)

During the time of my son's incarceration, I kept myself busy with my work and consistently watched sermons to stay upbeat and to stay in faith. My husband and I couldn't fall. We couldn't get weary because we were in a battle. Many days we asked God to renew our strength, especially around the holidays. As I was listening to a sermon by Pastor Joseph Prince on the righteousness of God, he explained that righteousness is not about right conduct but that it is a gift from God to us through Christ Jesus. He spoke about a young man who kept confessing that he was the righteousness of God and because of his confessions, things that were going so wrong in his life began to change and turn around and this young man had become very successful. Do we deserve righteousness? No! But it is a gift. So we should accept this gift and confess our righteousness every day. When we do this, all other things will be added unto us.

Although we fall, we fall into the hands of God. God is our righteousness. I spoke with my son every day and had him confess to me every day of his incarceration that he was the righteousness of God. His daily confession brought about a change in his heart, mind and soul. It also brought about a change in me. The more he (we) confessed this, the more I knew that it would strengthen his faith, and it did. He was eventually moved to the first faith-based prison in Georgia. While there, he attended Bible studies and worship services. He started a nightly prayer group with two other inmates and what started off with three people grew to over 30 men of all nationalities within months. Each night these men prayed for their families, sickness and diseases and justice. We heard testimonies from a few of the men about how God had moved in their lives once they learned forgiveness of themselves and others and began to stand on the Word of God. Fellow inmates would seek him out at his bunk for prayer and to study the revelation of God's word. They started calling my son's bunk "Bunk 57 Ministries" as a joke. Within three years we saw God move and my son was released.

A changed woman

A robber doesn't rob an empty house. The enemy comes to **steal, kill and destroy.** (John 10:10)

One morning, I was talking to another very good friend of mine. We were checking in with each other to see how the other was doing. She was battling health issues and I had just come home from a business trip. I shared with her that while on the trip, I was fighting a spirit of depression. It seemed that everything I had been praying for was not happening and that God was being silent. The enemy was constantly speaking to my mind that I wasn't good enough and that I was a fake and failure.

My friend said to me, "Karen, you know you got something in you when these spiritual battles come over you." She said, "A robber doesn't rob an empty house." Wow! Talk about a change in perspective. She went on tell me that I had so much in me that God was using and wanted to use, and therefore I was fighting this mental battle. She reminded me of battles I had already won and that if I didn't have God's Word and power in me, why would the enemy bother to try to stop me from walking in His fullness? Keep fighting with faith and prayer. My sisters, the enemy wants to keep us distracted and prevent us from fulfilling God's purpose. He definitely wants to stop our seed.

My son had to go through what he went through so God would get the glory. That blob I saw in my dream was a warning of the test to come, and God allowed things to happen so I would be prepared spiritually to fight. My son has so much power in him. The prison experience broke the barrier that was holding him back. He has since started a non-profit ministry called "Bunk 57 Ministries" that is now blessing young men and returning citizens. By faith, he is mentoring young men, teaching weekly Bible studies about discipleship and teaching citizens returning home how to be successful through entrepreneurship. His ministry is blessing so many with basic needs and connecting men with housing and jobs. What the devil meant for evil, God has turned around for His good. God promised through this journey that my eyes would see His glory, and I see it now.

Through this experience, I learned not be so judgmental of others. I learned that God has a purpose and a plan for us all if we will just allow Him to order our steps. I learned how to cast my cares on God because I was not and never would be in control. There was nothing I could do to help my son except to trust God to manage his life. I learned how to walk in forgiveness. If I did not forgive, I would keep myself imprisoned spiritually and God would not hear my prayers. I forgave myself, my son and the victim. I learned how to fight in faith. I learned how to be resilient. I learned that other people need me. They need me to share this story because they are going through similar or worse situations. They need to know that God is still alive and still works miracles. They need to know they are the righteousness of God and although our children stray, God can turn every situation around for our good.

Dedication

I dedicate this chapter to my Lord and Savior, to my husband Ira, to my mother, sister and brother who walked this journey with me and kept me encouraged, and to all the women who are walking through the fire with a child, but most of all to my son Ira Dubb, whose experience taught me the true fight of faith.

Kendall Scott is a Speech and Language Pathologist with more than twenty-five years of experience. Kendall's private practice "Happily Speaking", located in Warner Robins, GA, provides speech, language, alternative communication, feeding and swallowing, auditory and cognitive training, as well as fluency training, for populations birth to adult. "Happily Speaking" focuses on providing services for those who may not have access to quality services based on demographics. She proudly states, "I teach kids to talk back!"

Kendall received both Bachelor and Master of Science degrees in communication disorders from Nazareth College of Rochester, New York. As a member of the American Speech and Hearing Association and Sisters in Speech Therapy and Audiology, Kendall educates others, especially students of color, about her profession. She is also a proud member of Delta Sigma Theta Inc.

Kendall is a dynamic mother who loves deeply, a fierce loyal friend, and a trustworthy leader, who has found a niche in promoting political awareness and community involvement

TRUST AND OBEY

Kendall Scott

Honoring my typical morning routine, *Good Morning America* was playing in the background, while I sat up in my bed, thanking God for the canceled appointments. This would allow time for me to finish typing an evaluation report which was due the day before. As I hammered on the keyboard, the phone rang. I could see from the caller ID that it was Amanda, my line sister. "Good morning! What are you up to this morning? Have you started seeing clients?" I could hear her gleaming smile through the phone.

Isn't she at work? What has caused her to be so cheerful this morning? I curiously wondered. "I had a few cancellations so I'm up typing an evaluation report which was due yesterday," I muttered.

"Fantastic!" she bellowed, using the same smiling, cheerful voice. "I'm happy you're up getting it done; that's what we do." Then her voice tone dropped, "I have a proposition and you're probably going to say no but please hear me out."

I stopped typing. "Ok," I said.

"I think you need to get out of there. I know someone who's looking for a speech language pathologist here in Georgia, and I told them I knew an excellent one. I know you don't want to move to Georgia but the contract would be for one year; you can do anything for one year. My husband is being deployed so you could stay with us. It would be a win-win situation. We would help each other out." Then her voice tone changed back to the cheerful pitch, rising at the end of each sentence. "I think you should consider. Bye!" She hung up.

The laptop was now beside me. "Hell no, I don't want to go to Georgia, but I don't know if I want to stay here either," I thought aloud. It had been almost two years since my ex-husband left. The betrayal, villainous accusations, and my feelings of uncertainty—Amanda had observed all of this. I was at a crossroad. Having to figure out my life at almost 44 years old angered me. I had a plan before I got married at 35, and the plan did not include a husband, it did not include Upstate New York where I grew up, and it did not include Atlanta, Georgia. As a matter of fact, the plan was afoot when my ex pursued me, but when he shared his reluctance to move because of his children and being vested in his job, I placed the job searches and move on hold. We'd have ten years before the youngest of his children and my one child would be young adults, I reasoned. I could wait.

Fast forward, and here I was after eight years of marriage, divorced, my only child had gone to college, and the plan I put on hold at age 34 did not fit my life at age 44. My daughter called and I shared the conversation with her. "Mom, do it. I was planning on transferring and coming back home to go to school anyway. I will come see you instead of you coming to see me." She laughed. "Go mom, you don't have a reason not to. Auntie Mandy is right; it'll be good."

Taking advice from my then nineteen-year-old, I began prepping my resume. I didn't want to go to Georgia but needed to test the waters and get a feel for the job market. As a speech-language pathologist with twenty-two years' experience, my resume gained legs. Doesn't God grant the desires of your heart? Well, my desire was not to go to Atlanta, but I planned to move forward with the interview, praying, "Lord, you know I never liked Atlanta." A very quiet, yet pronounced voice replied, "I'm not sending you to Atlanta, I'm sending you to Middle Georgia." The answer lovingly chastened me. Humbled by what I had heard, my spirit agreed to obey, but my mind and body continued kicking and screaming. This, by far, was the most difficult battle.

Dr. Daryl Vining stated in his sermon one Sunday, "We can only see to the corner, but God sees around the corner. We must trust Him." There are numerous ways God has illustrated this for me. To start, my first trip to Georgia for the in-person interview was quite eventful. The rural school district was two and a half hours south of Atlanta. I seriously thought we had driven into an episode of *In the Heat of The Night*! What had I gotten myself into? I pondered. A grab bag of emotions came over me, but I kept moving forward and continued to talk to God throughout the interview and tour of the school and town. *Trust the Lord with all your Heart and lean not on your own understanding; In all your ways acknowledge Him, and he shall direct your paths.* Proverbs 3:5-6, NKJV. This verse was on re-play in my head. It was reassurance that God was in this and if I trusted Him, I would prevail.

My return flight was delayed, causing me to miss my connecting flight home. At first, being stuck in Charlotte infuriated me, then I changed my approach, deciding instead to be grateful that my godmother resided there. Going to her home allowed me to rest, schedule a new flight, arrange airport transportation, and secure a flight voucher for the inconvenience. Don't you know, two weeks later, I had to use that voucher to return to Georgia for a criminal background check. This was eye-opening and affirming. God made provisions for me by using the inconvenience of a missed flight. I needed to trust the process.

I arrived in Georgia and began working in September of 2016. Immediately it was apparent that I would have to find another stream of income. What had I done? Stress and dread came over me like a flood. I decided I'd become a provider with Georgia Medicaid and take on a few private clients. While meeting with a credentialing agent, she informed me of a place looking for a speech-language pathologist. "If you are interested, I'll pass your information along," she said. *Are you serious, God? Did you just...?* I often talk to God in my head simultaneously while doing other tasks or holding conversations. I was astounded and agreed that she could pass my information along to the pediatric speech clinic. I was employed within a week of that meeting. By October, I slowly began to rest in the Lord as I experienced His provision. The credentialing process was never completed for Georgia Medicaid, reportedly due to some red tape. None of it made sense at the time and I didn't care. God had provided another source of income. The money was consistent, and I was only staying through July.

By April 2017, I was at another crossroad. Amanda had learned that her husband was retiring. They decided to move to Athens so she could complete her doctorate degree. Instantaneously I was propelled into having to find a place to live and to consider staying in Georgia. I began looking into travel speech therapy positions, as they offered salary, housing, and incidentals. Nyla, a young woman whom I supervised during her graduate school externship, educated and guided me through the process. *Lord, if I get a travel position here in Middle Georgia, I'll stay; if not, I'll go home. Just make it clear.* Within two weeks offers in Middle Georgia came in. "Ok Lord, I'll stay a little longer, ten more months, and then I'm going to take an assignment elsewhere, and officially become a traveling SLP," I bargained.

Looking for an apartment was grueling. Besides the fact that I had never lived in an apartment, I did not know the area. Also, the location of the assignment had not been revealed. Talk about taking a shot in the dark. Settling on a place, I saw God's hand in this decision also. The location of the travel assignment wasn't revealed until two days before I started. My home was only fifteen minutes from the site and seven minutes from the pediatric clinic. Go God! "We can only see to the corner, but God sees around the corner. We must trust Him," noted Pastor Darryl Vining.

The season of 2017-2018 was challenging. I quit the travel assignment after four months. *Ok God, it's been over a year; it's time to go. I don't want to stay here.* While I was making plans to leave and never return, the pediatric clinic continued to proposition me to work full time. "No thank you," I replied. On November 15, 2017, they asked me if I would please consider covering a maternity leave. I literally rolled my eyes. "When?" I asked. "It would begin Monday, November 27," the director stated. *Are you kidding me, God—really?* This is me talking to God again during a conversation. The last day of the travel assignment was scheduled for November 22, which would provide time to reset and have employment without missing a beat. Most importantly, I would not have to break my lease or drive to New York during winter, I reasoned. Returning to the conversation with the director, I agreed to discuss the offer. I became a full-time employee at the pediatric therapy clinic on November 27, 2017 and remained there for the next three years.

During 2018, the itch to start a full-time private speech therapy practice returned. I went back to the credentialing agent, who informed me that processing my paperwork at that time would be a conflict of interest. My search for another firm fell flat. By October of 2018, I became depressed. I remember crying because I had no social life. I missed autumn in Upstate New York, the colorful fall foliage, and all things apples. "Why don't you go home?" friends would ask. "Why would you stay if you are miserable? You have an office in your house there, and you can go back to your job!" others would bellow. All of this was true, but I just felt like God was telling me to stay. I literally would hear a quiet voice during these conversations—quiet, yet it drowned out the commentary. The voice would say, "No." Tearfully, I obeyed. On my way to the laundromat one Saturday, I noticed a shop named 'Apple Basket.' I decided to stop in. Inside there was an assortment of gourmet caramel apples. A voice whispered, "Here you go, caramel apples— now what?" Fighting tears, I uttered "Thank you, Lord!" This was an overwhelming encounter with God demonstrating His love and care about every little detail of my life, including caramel apples.

I decided to seek counseling. Depression and anxiety were consuming me. *How can this be? I'm obeying the Lord by staying in Georgia, and I'm miserable.* The sermons at church became more poignant than ever. "Being in God's will is not always comfortable," was one of Pastor Darryl Vining's sermons. Covering bills in two states, how was I going to pay for therapy? I wondered. I reached out to a therapist recommended by a friend. The receptionist told me that they did not take insurance but before I hung up, she said "Wait—I have a question: Have you ever been assaulted or a victim of abuse?" I paused and answered, "Yes." She asked, "Do you have a police report?" I replied, "Yes." She instructed me to bring the police report, as I would qualify for free therapy services. Astounding! Another example where God used something that humans meant for evil for my good. In 2014 I was assaulted by my ex-husband's ex-wife. The embarrassment along with the emotional rejection and lack of support which followed was etched in my soul. Now four years later that assault opened the door to free therapy services. This is a true testament of the verse *All things work together for good to those who love God* (Romans 8:28, NKJV). Again, all I could do was praise. As I shared my struggles, pain, and unresolved issues, I mentioned that I wanted to start my own private practice but could not find a credentialing agent. The therapist gave me a recommendation. The person she recommended agreed to do my credentialing and became a good friend. Things were looking up.

"When we don't get the results we want, we want to quit on God" (paraphrased from one of Pastor Vining's sermons). There were several delays during the credentialing process. I became very discouraged and wanted to give up. My friend and brother Imari would constantly remind me, "If this was easy everyone would do it!" Sunday messages were hitting me like darts. "God did not put you on this earth to quit in the middle. Move with purpose and know where you are going. Put on your armor and know God will navigate your way." It took everything I had some Sundays to make it in the door of the church. When I arrived, God used messages such as these to keep me from losing heart. My plan was to leave the pediatric clinic before my next contract in November 2019, but I didn't have enough contracts or money for an office at that time.

In December 2019, I mustered up the courage to go to Dr .Tiffany Scandrett's office unannounced. She was an African American speech-language pathologist in the area who had her own speech therapy clinic. After introducing myself, I shared my plan to start my own clinic. I asked her if she would consider referring clients to me when she had an overflow, as I was just getting started. She looked at me and said, "I absolutely think you should start your own practice and I actually may have some clients for you." I was floored. At that time, Dr. Scandrett had been making changes to her schedule and had to move approximately ten families to a different provider. She told me that she would share my information with other providers, then she offered to be my mentor. Dr. Tiffany, as I call her, assisted me with finding office space and getting over the hump with the insurance contracts. She let others know that I was in the area and offered her office as a place for me to have a meet-and-greet. Dr. Tiffany cheered me on while holding me accountable. It was my time, but I could feel God saying, "Wait!" Again, I was very frustrated and just kept asking God "When?" Shoot, Dr. Tiffany started asking me, "When?" I remember telling her, "I don't know; I just have to wait." "Okay keep waiting," she said. Being my mentor, Dr. Scandrett counseled me on how there would never be the perfect time. She encouraged me to step out there. How I wanted to. It was very hard because I kept hearing God tell me to wait and I couldn't find a way to explain that.

Thanks to Dr. Tiffany, I started seeing my first private clients in January 2020. I wanted to leave the clinic but could not financially survive with the few clients I had. If you are faithful over a few things, He will make you ruler over many (Matthew 25:26). I held on to this promise. I worked approximately seventy hours weekly to build my clientele, but the progression was slow. I felt trapped. I stopped asking God why and began praying for a clear direction. In March of 2020, three months after I began seeing private clients and had signed a lease for $350.00 a month, the COVID-19 pandemic hit. The nation shut down. I was still working full time at the pediatric clinic, which qualified me for unemployment. During the shutdown, I was able to clear the slate for a clean break at the clinic and pour into my dream. I began to pound the pavement with marketing and requesting referrals. Operations commenced and the office was prepped. Had I not listened, had I not obeyed when God told me to wait, not only would I have not had the time to build my practice, but I would also not have gotten unemployment. I would not have been able to pay my bills. I would not have had anything and could have lost everything had I not waited. I coined my business name and had plans to open a full-time private practice in 2006. Looking back, I waited fourteen years. I kept getting started with a few clients, but never seemed to be able to operate full time independently. It took until July of 2020 for my practice to open, in a place I did not have on my radar. Looking in the rear-view mirror, had I not listened, had I not waited, had I not believed and trusted at various times during these fourteen years, I would have probably had to forfeit half of my practice to my ex-husband, as it would've been established during my marriage. With tears streaming down my face as I write these words, I thank God for protecting me. I thank God for making me wait! I thank God for making provisions. I have nothing but a heart filled with praise. It has not been easy, and it's still tough. It has been very uncomfortable, as I feel like a fish out of water and I miss my family, but I have a purpose and I'm fulfilling it. I'm in line with what God's plans are for me. I'm excited to see the blessings that will come.

Satan will tell you that it's over, but God knows the plans He has for you. We only miss out when we ignore what God tells us to do. When your dream is bigger than you are, God can make it happen. I am grateful to announce that my full-time private practice, Happily Speaking Speech Therapy Services, is open and thriving!

Dedication

For everyone who has questioned their position and God's timing, whose movements seem absurd to spectators, but you know you are following the still, quiet voice of the Lord.

Duquinha Thompson is a proud Cape Verdean from Boston, Massachusetts. Duquinha has lived in three states. She's went from Boston to Atlanta and now resides in Upstate New York with her husband and three children. She has a master's degree in mental health counseling and has owned and operated a licensed home daycare.

While living in Atlanta Duquinha had the opportunity to host a television show and be a part of a reality show that filmed and aired in Atlanta, Georgia. Duquinha has worked as a director for the past year and a half for a childcare resource and referral agency in the Syracuse area. Duquinha loves to spend time with her family and attend family gatherings. And when there is a babysitter, she enjoys date nights with her husband. She also enjoys quiet time to herself whether it's taking a walk, shopping, getting her nails done or just watching a good series on Netflix.

DEAR YOUNGER ME, YOU WILL HAVE THE VICTORY!

Duquinha Thompson

Vic-to-ry: the overcoming of an enemy or antagonist; achievement of mastery or success in a struggle or endeavor against odds or difficulties.

A pastor of mine once told me, "You better look in the mirror and tell that little girl that is in you that she is healed, she is set free, she's a grown woman now, and whatever she's been through doesn't define who she is and who she is becoming." That mirror is this chapter. My hope is that you as the reader can see my reflection through this chapter. This chapter is a little piece of me. It's short stories of Victory. It's how God used my relationships and experiences to shape the woman I am and the woman I am becoming.

The Beginning

I was born May 3, 1981 at Boston Medical Center. I arrived into the world causing my parents some distress and concern. The doctors told my mother and father that there looked like what appeared to be a tumor in my heart. I was fourteen days old when the doctors made the decision, with permission from my parents to perform open heart surgery. I cannot even imagine what my parents must have been feeling at the time. They had to put me in the hands of a doctor to perform such a scary procedure. But God must have had me in His hands performing his own miracle on my life. Turns out there was no tumor. Victory! I remember wearing a heart monitor periodically throughout elementary and middle school. I can recall my cardiologist saying to my mother, "Her heart has an extra beat but that's fine, we will continue to monitor her yearly." Well, I guess I must have a little extra love to share. Today I have a scar that begins under my right breast and runs across my back.

I grew up with a strong, resilient mother, a protective big brother, and an alcoholic father. I remember my father carrying me on his shoulders while he jogged and showing me love and affection with lots of hugs. But when he drank, he was different. My father was a hard worker. He drove a taxicab and would go to work as early as four in the morning. I guess you can say he worked hard and played hard. I was a little girl spending a lot of weekends anxiously waiting for my father to come home from being out all night. The weekends were never something I looked forward to. The bell would ring loudly. I can still hear it now, so clearly. I would lie in bed, startled, while I held onto my mother tightly as he made his way up the stairs. When he came in the room he would shout at my mother. My mother would plead for him to stop because my brother and I had school the next day.

I would go to school carrying that with me. I would find myself daydreaming a lot in school. In fact, I remember barely passing most of my classes because of my lack of focus. I was never told I was smart, nor did I ever feel smart. My brother was the smart one. I was just pretty. At least that's how I felt. At eleven years old

I began to use my diary to hold my thoughts, my secrets, my fears, my sorrows, my joy, hopes, and my dreams.

Here is my first diary entry (unedited)

Date: 6/16/92   Day: Tuesday

Dear Diary, Hi, my name is Duquinha. I am 11 years old, in the fifth grade. I am in school right now. We are cleaning because we only have two days for school left. Do you know who gave this diary to me? My aunt from Portugal. I just got you yesterday and I like you already! It's been nice talking to you, bye! See you!!! I go to St. Patrick school.

Date: 12-4-92   Day: Fri

Dear Diary,

Hi, today was a good day. I had fun at school but right now isn't a very good time because my mother and father are fighting—not really fighting but now yelling because my father had an affair with a woman and my mother told me she was sorry she married the wrong guy. Every day I have to listen to this. I am sick of this. I hope one day my mother and father separate but I will still get to see my father, and I would like to stay with my mother because she gives me everything. My father gives me things too but mothers are close. They're still yelling at each other. I wish this would stop one day. Bye, see you tomorrow. ☹

Date: 2/8/94   Day: Wed

Dear Diary,

Hi, it's me. I am in bed. I didn't have school because of the weather. Yesterday was the worst day of my life.

My mom and dad were in an argument and my mother was screaming and crying. She fainted and my brother got water and my father put it on her. They are getting a divorce. My stomach hurts so I'll tell you the reason later.

My parents divorced when I was fourteen years old. Amongst the unpleasant memories there were many good ones. We had family gatherings every holiday, Barros family reunions every year, and yearly family vacations to Maine, Martha's Vineyard and New Hampshire. I have memories of getting wet by the fire hydrant, and playing Double Dutch outside during the summer, and many sleepovers with cousins. I was in dance and my brother was in karate. My mother worked hard to keep us out of trouble and gave us a Catholic school education. My brother always protected me. In fact, he is the one who had "the talk" with me. This is what he said after he asked me to take a seat: "All boys want is one thing, and that's sex. Don't trust them, don't talk to them, respect yourself, and by the way, they don't respect you." I did just the opposite. I didn't respect myself or my body and I didn't see my full worth. Instead, I was attracted to men who acted just like my brother and father. The men I liked were popular, players, charismatic men, the "bad boys." They say a daughter's first glance of how a man should treat her is how her father treats her mother. God bless my brother for trying.

Date: 9/20/94   *Day: Mon*
Dear Diary, Today it wasn't so bad at school. There's a new boy in my class. Warren is his name. I think he likes me. He keeps on looking at me. Oh well! I don't like him; he's not my type! That's all I have to say. He's cute!

The first boy I ever fell for was a drug dealer. We were fifteen when we met at the Boys and Girls club. He sold marijuana and cocaine on a street corner. He was popular, and he was a "bad boy." I swear his mother prayed I would end up his wife. God had other plans. Thank you, Jesus! Off and on for five years I was emotionally invested in someone who hardly called me, who never took me out on a date, who didn't respect me as I should have been respected. While he was visiting me in my college dorm one evening, he went through my diary, saw something he didn't like, and smacked me in my face. He immediately apologized. That was the first and last time he did that. Thank God that He delivered me from that situation. ***Victory!***

Atlanta and Faith

Date: 10/13/2004

    Dear diary, I cannot believe I did it—I moved to Atlanta, Georgia, just got up and moved and without much thought. It's been a challenge and every day brings on a new one. It's been a good challenge. I've been born again and am finally discovering me! And it's been a beautiful thing. The past doesn't even matter anymore; all is new. I feel great on the inside. Appearance on the outside is not so important anymore. My spirit rules the outside appearance and that's what's important. I discovered there is so much that I am capable of doing. In the name of Jesus, I ask that you please help me shine and speak to people through you so that the world can recognize you and worship you.

My friend and I officially moved to Atlanta, Georgia, January 2004, after college graduation. One of my most precious and transformational moments while living in Atlanta was joining a church and becoming saved. **Victory!** I grew up going to Catholic church all my life. I knew this was different. I'd never seen people raising their hands while shouting, unless they were in a dance club. They were shouting and praising Jesus. I remember during one service, I looked over at a young lady. The young lady had her eyes closed, shouting, praising, and singing. I couldn't bring myself to do the same. I felt embarrassed. I thought to myself, *How cool it would be if one day I can praise the way she praises.* The eleven months that I lived in Atlanta is when my faith was the strongest. I was excited. I knew that with God anything was possible and every day I could not wait to see what He had in store for me.

Notes from Sunday service   *Date: 10/10/04*
"Anything done out of fear doesn't last." It's only when you let go of what people think of you that you become the greatest you can be. Go where faith leads you.

Oprah's cousin: girl, he's not the one!

It was Easter Sunday and my roommate and I were walking out of church service. It was a good word. A brown-skinned young man approached my roommate and me. He introduced himself as Oprah's cousin, after he said his name. He also mentioned that he worked making music beats for a famous R&B group, all while attending Morehouse. From there on out my roommate and I got into parties, events, and clubs, in VIP only. We walked right in with the R&B group. They took us in as if we were family. We weren't groupies, I promise. I remember going to an event hosted by the R&B group. There were two women arguing over the brown-skinned young man. He sat there watching and I observed. Here I go again making bad decisions in men, choosing to take interest in someone who wasn't interested or invested in me. I felt hurt. I felt like I wasn't seen by this young man. I didn't understand why God couldn't hurry up and bless me with someone who would love me, someone who would respect me, and someone who would one day marry me. He was waiting on me to see my own worth. Well, at least I met his cousin, Oprah!

Notes from Sunday service   *10/9/2004*

"There are things God wants to do in you and for you before that someone comes in."

"When that person comes you want the wall repaired and ready for him."

"The Enemy will try to show you all the setbacks of being single."

Spotlight

My roommate and I went out one evening. A young man stepped up to me and told me about a show they were putting together. "It's a version of America's next top model but ATL style." There were fifteen of us ladies. We met every other day for early morning workouts; we had fashion shows and photo shoots. We were down to three ladies. It was the day a winner was picked. "And the winner is Duquinha!" they announced. I was pleasantly surprised. **Victory!** It was during a fashion show for "America's next top model, Atlanta style" that I was noticed by a producer. This producer was looking for a host for his new show called *Detail TV*. He said that there was "something different about you." He asked me if I wanted to be the host. I said, "Yes." with hesitation. Me? A host? He picked me? My faith was through the roof at this time. I believed that God was sending me all the opportunities and I wasn't even looking for them. I prayed, I believed, I was living through my faith. I interviewed a few celebrities and hosted several events. It was quite the experience. I remember being very nervous before interviewing these celebrities. I would pray, pace, practice, prepare, and perform. You never know what God is doing for you behind the scenes. *Victory!*

Trust in the Lord with all your heart and lean not on your own understanding; in all your ways submit to him, and he will make your paths straight. Proverbs 3:5, NIV

Back home again

I moved back to Boston after eleven months of living in Atlanta. I was back where it all began, Boston, my childhood home. My plans were to work, save, and move back to Atlanta. But God had other plans. Out of the blue one day I received a phone call from someone I briefly dated while I was in Atlanta. Eventually, we were in a long-distance relationship that lasted two years. One day he asked me to marry him. I reluctantly said yes. His plan was to enlist in the army, marry me, take me to Germany, and get all the benefits from the army that came from being married. I never met any of his friends or family members. I should have known that was a red flag. He would borrow money from me for bills because in his eyes, I was obligated. After all, I put my name on his apartment rental and on his Verizon phone bill. At one point he even asked my mother for several hundred dollars. I was blinded. I didn't see the signs. I remember visiting him in Atlanta and going through his things. I came across a black bag full of women's underwear. Ugh. What was that about? Who was I dealing with? He had an excuse, of course. He had a conversation with me one day and stated that he didn't know what ethnicity he was. In fact he lied; he said he was someone he was not. I was confused and hurt and yet I was relieved. I realized that he was not meant for me. *Victory!*

After staying with my mother for several months and concluding that I didn't have enough privacy, I moved to my own apartment outside of Boston. I still felt like something was missing. I felt lonely in that apartment. I continued to go out partying with friends on the weekends. While trying to fill a void, I became pregnant for the first time at twenty-five years old. I didn't feel ready. I was scared. This wasn't what I pictured being a mother would look like for me. I cried. I wept. I was in disbelief and felt overwhelmed. With sleepless nights and a lot of hesitation, I decided that I would have an abortion. It was shortly before I turned twenty-six and a few weeks before Mother's Day when I had the abortion. Mother's Day came along and that's when I began to imagine what it would have been like if I decided to keep my baby. I had shame, I felt guilty, and I had a whole lot of regret! I lay in my bed in my apartment, alone, one night, crying out to God. I asked him to forgive me; I hated what I did. If only I could take it back, I would have. As I lay there watching television, changing channels, and crying, I came across a pastor. The pastor pointed and said these words: "There is someone out there who had an abortion. God has forgiven you, he loves you, and you are forgiven." I knew in my heart that message was for me. **Victory!**

Building my faith—God's Plan

I started going to Jubilee Christian Church after visiting several other churches in Boston. I wanted my relationship with God once again. I wanted to be excited again about what God was doing. When I found Jubilee, I knew that was my church! I was twenty-seven and a single mother. My daughter was born in 2008. She changed my perspective; it was no longer about me. She slowed me down. From the moment she was born it was about me and her. Her father was there from the day she was born but not there for me during my nine months of pregnancy. He made it clear that he was not ready for the commitment that I so desperately wanted but didn't know I deserved. Once again, I was hurt. But I had my daughter, and I had my faith. Although I loved my church, it was big. I wanted to feel more connected. So I became an official member and began to serve as a gate keeper. My job as a gate keeper was to usher people to their seats. By no means did I picture myself wearing that uniform and being visible to the whole congregation as they walked in for Sunday service. The uniform just wasn't cute enough. But God had his own plans. It was 2012 on New Year's Eve, I was in service and prayed out to God for a husband, and for my own family. It was that year that I met my husband. I was serving one Sunday when he spotted me. He was checking me out. In his words, "It was your spirit that I was attracted to." Sure, it was. We went to the same church for about five years, but we never actually saw one another until I started serving.

He never approached me in church but waited until he saw me on a date with another gate keeper at Panera Bread. After scoping the scene, he approached us and introduced himself as the pastor's armor bearer. I didn't see him until two months later, again at Panera Bread. This time I was alone. He approached me, asked me what happened to the guy I was on the date with. I told him he wasn't my type. He said, "He fumbled, and I picked it up." He was confident, talkative, and told me his life story within twenty minutes. He told me about his six-year-old son, that he was from New York, and that he worked in sales. I shared that I was a single mother, and that I had my own home childcare business. Before he left, he gave me his card. I was hesitant. I thought to myself, *Oh God, here we go again. Another date, another man, another disappointment.* I had to protect myself from being hurt. I had been single and celibate for two years, and I wasn't going to let just anyone into my circle anymore.

We spoke every day and had long conversations. We dated, we held hands, and we took long walks. I met his son; he met my daughter. His son was dribbling a basketball outside my workplace. He was tall for a six-year-old. His dad was so proud. My daughter was on the beach when she first met him. She gravitated toward him. I couldn't believe it. She didn't like anyone. I knew he was different from the other men I had dealt with in the past. He saw my worth, he treated me the way I always wanted to be treated. I made him work for me, which is something I never did with anyone else. I remember him telling me that he never worked so hard to get a girl. After four months of dating, he told me, "God said you're my wife." I thought to myself, *This man is crazy because God didn't tell me that.* My walls admittedly went up. I was so used to being mistreated that I almost let my future husband go, and only because I was afraid of really being loved.

My pastor told me to either let him go or realize the type of man that was in front of me. We got married in 2014. *Victory!* We got baptized together and became deacons at our church. *Victory!* My husband Keith and I had our first son together after suffering a miscarriage. *Victory!* Our son was in the NICU for 10 days after we both had high blood pressure. I had Bell's palsy after I gave birth to my son. The right side of my face was numb. My lip drooped when I spoke. God healed me. *Victory!* Three years later we had our daughter, but not before we suffered two miscarriages. Our daughter's due date was November 1. God had other plans. She was born two months early and on her dad's birthday, September 16. I stayed in the hospital for three weeks before giving birth to her. She stayed in the NICU for two weeks before we brought her home. *Victory!* We now have a blended family of six!

God has always shown His love even when I didn't see it, when I couldn't recognize it and when I thought I didn't deserve it. He never fails and He always has shown up on time. That little girl who was hurt, sad, and lonely, that young lady who chose the wrong men and didn't see her worth, is grown up now. She carries with her pieces from her childhood, broken pieces. She carries great childhood memories as well. She's been hurt, confused, and lonely. She's had victory, triumphs, and successes. She wouldn't be who she is now without all those experiences. She is a work in progress. She is not perfect and still has a lot to learn about herself. She is a masterpiece that has yet to be finished.

For I know the plans I have for you, declares the LORD, plans to prosper you and not to harm you, plans to give you hope and a future. Jeremiah 29:11, NIV

Date: August 22, 2021

Dear younger me,

you will have the VICTORY! You will go through some childhood trauma; you will have a lot of love in your childhood as well. Always remember, the love you had, and the constant encouragement you received from your mother, the protection from your brother, and the wise counsel from your father. Carry those good memories with you. You will make a few bad choices in men. It will take a few heartbreaks to realize you are worth more than you think. Don't worry, you will get your own version of your Cinderella story. It may not look exactly how you pictured it to happen or come when you want. Be patient. It will be worth the wait! You will grow up to be a wife and a mother one day, just like you've dreamt. You will question yourself, your strength, and your ability from time to time. Remember who your father is in heaven. You are fearfully and wonderfully made. Everything you've kept in your journals, everything you've been through, has led you to this moment. Don't forget to love yourself. Take care *of yourself. Remember to see things for what they are. Don't believe the lies your own self tells you. Know the truth. The truth is that God loves you. The truth is that you're not perfect and you never will be. So don't even try. Dream big, then chase your dreams. Write that book, tell your story! Love hard. Live on purpose. Don't be afraid to let your light shine. Be yourself. Show your beauty from inside to outside. Don't dim your light for anyone! This, of course, won't be easy. It will be a journey. Stay prayed up. Keep God close. Love with all your heart. Let your walls down but not just for anyone. Make them work for it. You're worth it! Your worth is immeasurable. Be transparent. Be you. ☺*

Love, Your older self.

Dedication

This book is dedicated to all the little girls who will one day become women, and to all the women who are healing from the broken little girl who is in them. For the mothers of daughters, I pray that we see our daughters as their own individual selves. Their stories will be written differently because the little girls within their mothers are being healed.

To my mother, thank you for your constant encouragement, tough love, and strength.

LaTia N. S. Russell, LCSW is a wife, mother, and co-captain of a multi-generational household. LaTia is an Amazon Best-selling author, licensed clinical social worker and certified grief recovery specialist. She is the co- author of "Live in Color" a positive affirmation coloring book for children, created with her 4-year-old son and husband.

LaTia has a B.A in Psychology from Hampton University. A Master's of Social Work degree from Loyola University-Chicago, and is currently pursuing her Doctorate of Social Work (DSW) degree from the University of Alabama (Roll Tide)! You can find LaTia traveling and dodging, being kicked in the head from the demonstrations of her 4-year-old son's acrobatic stunts (according to CJ, he is a real-life Ninja…his Ninja skills have not been vetted). LaTia and her husband have created Ties That Bind Publishing, LLC, their family-owned publishing agency. They can be found at ties that bind publishing (everywhere)!

THROUGH THE FIRE

LaTia Russell

They say there's nothing like a mother's love. I'm not quite sure who "they" are or what type of tools they used to measure a mother's love compared to other types of love, but I can tell you, there was a time in my life I would've argued this sentiment with conviction. I'm not sure what long-standing generational curse (or perceived) curse there is on the Black mother and Black daughter relationship, but I'm here to share that by the grace of God, my mother and I were able to work our way through the fire and emerge in a state where we can talk about our journey. I'm not even going to sugarcoat it for you—the journey was long; it was ugly, painful, pitiful, depressing... but GOD!

Initially, when I was brainstorming what I would write about, I thought I would talk about some very specific traumas I endured. However, whenever I thought about sitting down to write, I just couldn't and therefore, these pages remained blank. I knew I was up against the clock, and one evening while lying in bed, I heard my mom and son engaging in their "GiGi" and grandson banter. It hit me like a ton of bricks: It's not just my story I'm supposed to tell, it's ours, my mother's and mine. Even after feeling pretty confident about my task, I still had to sit with this idea a bit longer because it's one thing to air my own traumas and triumphs but involving my mom means I'll also be telling her story. Simply put, there is no me without her, and our stories are so deeply intertwined that in every scenario of me talking about my life story, she would be written in.

So one evening after she returned home from work, she came into our (my husband's and my) room and we were chatting about this and that. I took that opportunity to get her permission to tell her story. I shared with her the project I'm working on, and our mission to inspire. I expressed that it comes to a point where, for some reason, mothers and daughters seem to disconnect, and the relationship suffers greatly. I won't get into the history or speculations of why this is because that's not why we're here. I just know that in the Black community, I've often heard that a shift happens with mothers and their expectations of their daughters versus their sons. And not like this is a brag or anything, but this was not one of my mother's and my barriers to overcome since I'm her only child. Please trust me when I say our battles were a-plenty.

A bit about my amazing mother: She is the fourth child of eight, smack-dab in the middle of the pack. Her mother and father were married but later divorced and unfortunately, her father was absent in her life. Please know that I will only be speaking specifically about my mother because I've not sat down with my aunts and uncles to query them about their perceived childhood experiences and personal relationships with their parents. Growing up, my mother was extremely independent. She completed high school, worked, bought her own vehicles and did the big sister thing with style and grace. I never heard her or anyone ever mention that she experimented with drugs or had any issues with alcohol. She had a straight head on her shoulders and was living and loving life. She was black girl magic before there was a description of what black girl magic was.

My mom was a fantastic roller-skater and would frequent the local roller rink and the surrounding area roller rinks. It was there that she met my father (may he rest in peace). They were in their early 20s and living life. My mom shared that it was my father who introduced her to drugs and once that introduction happened, she "took to it like a duck to water" (Barbara Williams). My parents were 22-23 when they had me. We lived in an apartment and then my childhood home. I know for a fact that I was about the age of three, nearing four, when my mom left. I have very early memories of my mom living in my childhood home, but they are few. A particular memory I have is of my parents arguing in our kitchen. My dad was shirtless, and my mom slapped him in the back. I can't say she left immediately after that; I just know that is the last memory I have of her in our home.

So there we were, my father and I. He was not even 30, with a toddler daughter and the mother of his child gone from their home. My parents were never a couple again. My first day of kindergarten, I remember my dad walking me to school. My mother was not there. From kindergarten to fourth grade, I lived with my dad. I'm unable to recall many memories of my mother during that time. I do remember that she bounced around from here to there, staying with friends until she and her boyfriend moved in together. If I'm being completely honest, so much of that time from my childhood I've blocked out. One thing that is embedded in my memories is that during a very crucial time in my development, my mom was not there. As I'm standing and looking back, this would continue to be a consistent theme throughout my life.

Now, don't get me wrong, I would see my mother here and there. I would spend some weekends with her, and I specifically remember this to be true in the third grade. This time period stands out because I broke my wrist in the third grade and remember my blue cast and visiting my mom at her friend's house on the weekends. I also remember going to court with my mother once, and her being taken away in handcuffs. I ended up going back to the judge's chambers and having to call someone to come and pick me up. My mother spending time incarcerated is also a very vivid memory of my childhood. She was not only using drugs but began selling them as well. The combination of the two set my mom, and ultimately me, on a very tumultuous path.

I remember telling my dad that I wanted to go and live with my mom when I was in the fifth grade. So for the fifth, sixth and most of seventh grade, I was "with" my mom. During fifth grade, my mom and I lived with her long-time boyfriend. In the sixth grade, my mom and I moved in with my grandmother. There was a time during the sixth grade where my mom was incarcerated. I remember going with my grandmother down to the county jail to visit her—the same county jail I would work in decades later as a Licensed Clinical Social Worker. My mom did end up going to prison for a short time. I spent that time living with my grandmother. When my mom was released from prison, I returned to live with her and her long-time boyfriend.

During this period of our lives, I remember praying so hard for my mother. I was terrified that she would die and go to hell because of her lifestyle. As a child, I had ulcers and remember my dad saying to me once, "Little girl, you are too young to be carrying the weight of the world on your shoulders." Unfortunately, I didn't know how to be anyone else. People coming in and out of our home was the norm. I recall being in my mom's bedroom and seeing a small glass with white powdered lines on it. It's important for me to note that I've never seen my mother ingest a single narcotic. I also never saw her complete a drug transaction in front of me, despite the fact that it was happening all around me.

There was another time I remember living with my mom. I was sitting in our apartment on the living room floor. I believe I was in the seventh grade, and I was completing geography homework. The police kicked in our doors and raided our apartment. I remember them tearing my room apart and every adult in that space lying face down on the floor in handcuffs. I ended up back with my grandmother. It was in junior high school that I started my menstrual cycle, and my mother was behind bars. My younger cousin and I went to the grocery store with my grandmother, and because I was too embarrassed and no one had really talked with me about what to do when you start your period, I tried choosing a sanitary napkin and sneaking it into the shopping cart. Obviously, my grandmother saw (because she was paying for the grocery items), and we went back to get the correct items. When my mother was released from her incarceration this time, I remember she would pop up from time to time but never for any length of time.

For a short time in the eighth grade, I lived with my mom and her long-time boyfriend. Eighth grade stands out to me because I remember this year in particular, I felt so sad all of the time. It was in the eighth grade that I would write my first batch of poems (that I subsequently ripped up in anger). I also remember coming home after school and drinking NyQuil even though I was not sick. I believe my mother ended up back behind bars, and I went back to finish out my eighth-grade year with my grandmother. Nearing the end of the eighth grade, I decided to go back and live with my dad. I was excited to be headed to high school and was even more excited that both of my parents would be able to see me graduate from junior high. My mom didn't show up to my graduation or my graduation party. I was crushed but had resolved myself to the fact that this was nothing new. Sadly, I was used to her letting me down and not being there when I needed her the most.

As I entered high school, so much of the back and forth is a blur. What is crystal clear is that I yearned for the love of my mother, her physical presence, and she could not give that to me. If I were to ask my 14-year-old self how she was feeling at this time, I'm 100% sure she would tell me "abandoned & embarrassed." I would see some of my friends and their mothers and would be so sad. Again, this is not to brag, but because in a way, I was forced to tough it out and grow up pretty fast, I was able to cherish the moments I did have with my mom, when I had them. I also knew that she overcompensated with material things because she was unable to give me what I needed emotionally. However, that didn't make the emotional void hurt any less.

I lived with my dad, stepmother, and baby sister in my childhood home throughout high school. My stepmother's son would return home from time to time. During high school, I would go and spend weekends intermittently at my mom's house with her new boyfriend. With the exception of her being "free" for a longer period of time, not much had changed. For the most part, my mom was still fully cemented in the world of drugs. My sophomore year of high school, my father was diagnosed with stomach cancer. It would be an uphill battle for him. I remember getting chicken pox that year and having to go and stay with my mom during that time since my dad's system was immunocompromised because of the cancer and his treatments. My dad's cancer went into remission, I was able to go back home, and our weekend routine continued.

There was a time where I tried to talk to my mom about all of the things—tried to express how I felt and how much pain I was in from her simply not being there. I can't say that I remember exactly all that was said, or my tone. I do remember my mom slapping me, and me thinking "the audacity" of her to put her hands on me after all that she'd put me through. I'd already become a master of bottling up my feelings; this was just the super glue added to the bottle. I remember being over at my mom's house one weekend, sitting in the living room watching TV and hearing a knock at the door. I went to answer the door, and there stood two plainclothes detectives. Once again, I witnessed my mother being walked away in handcuffs. I called my dad, and he came to pick me up. It was this same year that my dad's cancer returned, and he passed away. My mother was in prison.

Graduating from high school was surreal because I honestly didn't believe I was able to muster through. I'd always been good in school, achieved good grades, honor roll, dean's list, etc; however, this was different. Even with all of the love and support around me from my extended family, I felt like an orphan. My father was deceased, and my mother was in prison on the day that I walked across the stage to receive my high school diploma. I did not visit my mother in prison this time around, and I don't remember speaking with her very often. I do remember writing her a very LONG letter, which, in hindsight probably wasn't the smartest thing to do since I aired it all out—everything!

I began college without my parents. And so much of my survivorship and resiliency was wrapped up into the fact that growing up, I had a mother who was consistently absent, using and selling drugs. There were two very pivotal moments in my young womanhood that tried to shatter me into pieces. In high school, I was raped. After it happened, I went to my mom's house because I knew she wouldn't ask a lot of questions. I did tell her what happened. She did her best to be there for me, but the bridge was already too long and wide for it to mean anything other than words. In college, my freshman year, someone I trusted violated me in an unforgivable way, and no one protected me. My mom was still incarcerated at the time.

My mother was released from prison the summer of my freshman year in college, going into my sophomore year. She returned home, obtained a job, got back on her feet and I'm proud to say that she's never looked back. That was the summer of 2000. She and I began talking a bit more frequently once she returned home, but whenever I came home for breaks, I came back to my childhood home and stayed with my stepmother and little sister. Before my dad passed away, he asked me to stay there, and so I did, as my way to honor him. My mom and I were trying to find our footing—our new normal, if you will. Since I fully believe in transparency, I'm going to be completely honest. We had no bond. There was no relationship.

Deep down inside, I was still the toddler that she left, the little girl who'd seen her taken away in handcuffs numerous times, the pubescent/teenage girl navigating major life milestones without the guidance of her mother. We missed out on the opportunity to build an attachment and healthy relationship when she left me all those years ago. So we were both literally and figuratively at crossroads. How did we get back what never was, but also not become a part of the growing number of struggling mother/daughter relationships? To her credit, my mother never stopped trying, ever. We did our best to talk more. She apologized until she couldn't apologize anymore.

I knew I was going to have to do some soul searching to determine if I was going to meet her halfway. I desperately wanted to; I really didn't know how. I didn't know how to fully let go of the hurt, anger, resentment and sadness I felt for the years lost. My mother never gave up; she kept walking her path. She kept showing up and being a constant in my life. She traveled to Hampton, VA to see me receive my degree from (the REAL HU) Hampton University. When I returned back home after college and moved into my first apartment, she was there. When I went back to graduate school to get my Master's of Social Work degree, and my very first car was on its last leg, she was there. Graduating my Master's program, she was there. Getting married, she was there. When my PaPa, my paternal grandfather, passed away, she was there—never pushy, just the constant that I needed, exactly when I needed.

My mom moved in with my husband and me over 10 years ago, not because she needed to, but I really think God knew that she and I needed her to. We needed to share the same space to continue to build and nurture our relationship. And, if I'm still being honest, even though things were on the right path for us, there was a piece of me that couldn't shake that last bit of ick I felt. I would find myself respectfully quietly challenging things she'd say or tell me. She would genuinely be mothering me and a part of me was not having it. It wasn't until I became certified as a grief recovery specialist and did some grief work on our relationship that I was finally able to surrender all of the ick.

Although my mom and I have been "through the fire," I wholeheartedly believe we both are who we are as a result of our tumultuous journey. If resilient was a relationship, it'd be ours. I'm so proud to share that my dear mother continues to remain a constant for me. Seeing her build an amazingly loving and healthy relationship with her grandson gives me all of the feels. Our journey remains because all relationships require work, but I'm deeply committed to ensuring ours is a tale for the ages, a testament of what it looks like when you simply stay the course.

Dedication

1 Peter 4:8, ESV

Above all, keep loving one another earnestly, since love covers a multitude of sins.

First and foremost, this chapter is dedicated to our creator, for seeing fit to see us through the fire. To my AMAZING mother, Barbara Williams, if I could allow you to look into my heart, you would see my scars from the past have been healed and covered with your love from so many yesterdays. To know that I am the woman I am because of the woman you are makes my soul smile. Your strength, courage and resilience leave me in awe. I am SO proud of you. I'm proud to be your daughter and that God saw fit to bless me with you, through it all. I love you immensely and will proudly state it in every dedication that I can, because the world needs to know what this type of love looks like. This chapter is dedicated to every mother and daughter fighting for a genuinely loving and healthy relationship. Stay the course because you deserve to love one another without strongholds or limits.

All of my Love, Tia

"True forgiveness is when you can say, 'Thank you for that experience'."

Oprah Winfrey

Born and raised in Brooklyn, New York, **Rukiya Rice** has always had a passion for the arts, specifically dance. She spent her Middle School-College years studying dance, music and theatre. She trained in rigorous programs such as Creative Outlet dance theatre of Brooklyn, Alvin Ailey and Dance theatre of Harlem. In her passionate pursuit of the arts in college at the American Musical Dramatics Academy, she had no idea that would lead her in relationship with Jesus.

After the loss of her late mother at the age of 19, Rukiya said yes to Jesus at the age of 20. Completing her Bachelor of Fine Arts in Dance, she had no idea that God had plans to use her outside of her comfort and understanding, which would be beyond her degree. Rukiya has served in ministry and Youth development for the past five years. Her heart is after serving communities that she grew up in, along with serving communities through preaching the gospel. She looks forward to using her testimony as an opportunity to draw young women, men and adults to the love and salvation of Jesus Christ for their lives.

PROMISCUITY TO PROMISE

Rukiya Rice

Born and raised in Brooklyn, New York, in 1995 to be exact, it is safe to say I am a part of one of the coolest generations ever—the 90s. Many would probably argue with me because I was a baby in the 90s, not really having an opportunity to live during that era. I would still argue back that I am a 90s baby. Now why is it important for you to know this? There's something special that we 90s and 2000s babies experienced during our developmental stages. We were introduced during a time where technology, fashion, music, media and many more things were taking a turn in a way we had no idea was coming. Social media had taken its peak by the time I hit middle school. Sites such as Sconex and MySpace are where I saw a lot of my peers honored for fashion/creativity and sometimes even exploited unwillingly about their sexual behaviors. Gadgets such as MP3 players and iPods introduced sites such as Lime-wire, where free music was accessible to download for these gadgets. With the privacy of just me and my headphones, I fed myself music from artists such as Trey Songz, Vybz Kartel, Keyshia Cole, Tynesha Kelly and many more. These artists taught me more about life, relationships, sex and people than I learned from actual family/friends. Who would have thought that a 13-year-old would learn to desire sexual relations or even love relationships through songs like *Scratching me up* and *I should've cheated*. The list can continue of the many forms of influence that shaped my young, perverted mind—so much so that I had no idea it would follow me into the traumas, decisions and mind of my adult years.

If I'm honest, that seed of lust, promiscuity and also identity in those things did not begin there. Instead, it began in my own home at the age of six. Growing up in the 2000s there was an increase of porn that would air on cable television but at a certain hour when children my age shouldn't be awake. This six-year-old, however, admittedly had to use the bathroom in the middle of the night. After my trek to the bathroom, I returned to my room to flip through channels before I fell back asleep. I came across a show called "Girls Gone Wild." These women would be flashing their breasts as a sense of enjoyment, while men applauded them because of this action. That was the day I began to desire to touch myself based on these images. Before I continue with my story, I believe it's important to know that we have an enemy of our soul, and that he's Satan himself. It was his very plan to pollute my innocent mind with images of naked women and use that to pervert my purity. Imagine not knowing anything about what purity is or the fact that it can be taken away by exposure to one thing at six while looking for cartoons to put you back to bed at 2 a.m. Satan, knowing the call on my life before I even had any exposure to it, wanted to kill, steal and destroy it. His plan was to destroy it through sexual per-version. From that day on, I struggled secretly with masturbation, pornography, same-sex attraction and premature sex with boys/men. In fact, at the time, I didn't even acknowledge it as something I struggled with. In second grade, a friend of mine at the time and I were in the girl's bathroom discussing the same images we had both discovered in the night hours and attempted to touch each other, to recreate that same stimulation in our private areas that we created for ourselves in secrecy.

It amazes me that many young men and women actually go through this kind of stage. Adults and the world around us either tell us we are being "fast, too grown" or we will be told to sit our tails down. Other conversation would let us know that this is natural, that it is ok to be experiencing such sexual urges at a certain age; it's called puberty. Missing in fact is that it's all the agenda of the enemy of our soul to keep us trapped in cycles that will essentially keep us from the purpose of God on our lives. My virginity was not the thing that changed because of a hymen breaking, my virginity was in fact stolen at the age of six when I was exposed to sexually impure images for my soul.

Fast forward to the age of 16, when I lost my "hymen" virginity. It was done "right," at least from my own standards and not God's. The young man was my boyfriend, we were both virgins, and from my perspective we cared for/trusted one another. In my ignorance, I did not know that I was just creating a deeper soul tie with this spirit of lust and perversion. Now I wouldn't say that I was one of those young ladies who lost her virginity and from then went on a sex spree; I had a bit more class than that. Plus, as I had mentioned previously, I've seen peers of mine be exploited on "slut pages" by young men who didn't value their bodies, essentially because these young women didn't value themselves. My fear was to never be seen as that, because once again, I believed that this was something that only I went through, so I needed to keep this as secretive as possible. My thoughts of sex had been so perverted I believed that it was always connected to me liking someone. I never took the time to know people outside of our bodies being connected. I began to see this pattern of relationships I found myself in and out of. These relationships would always end in heartache, snatching pieces of me that I didn't think would be returned. This was acceptable in this day and age. We were teenagers; we would crush on people, get to know them; our friends would know their friends, and it would become a whole thing. Even if penetration was never involved, soul ties come in many forms. Just as I was a young woman who was exposed to things prematurely, there were many other young men and women who were operating out of this same brokenness we knew nothing about.

A few years later, I was 19 living in LA as a full-time college student working on my degree. I received grievous news that my mother had passed away and I needed to come home immediately. Just when you thought this girl wasn't broken enough, I then was hit with this. I didn't have the privilege of seeing my mother every day up until that moment like my other sisters and family had. The touch of her hand and closeness of her skin had not been experienced by me for four months, until I faced her in her casket. If I didn't use relationships, sex, weed and alcohol before, I assure you it was going to be my comfort now. Upon my arrival back in New York after receiving the news, there was a question I had for God, the universe, Jesus, myself or whomever I thought would listen to me at that time, that was very essential in me continuing in this thing called life. I remember vividly stating that there must be a bigger purpose to this and asking why I still existed.

Little did I know that such a sincere inquiry would stir the spirit of the one and only Holy and Righteous God to begin to pursue me in ways I would never be able to resist. In my pursuit of knowing that truth, I still continued with what I knew best: masturbation, porn, sex, weed, drinking—all the things that would contribute to me running away from my problems. What I thought was simple enjoyment actually took me farther away from true healing. I started to research astrology and spirit guides, manifestation of spirits speaking to me, in great hunger to know the why of my mother passing and the why of my existence on earth. I had no idea that it would be Jesus who would burst his way into my life and provide all the truth, healing and guidance I was in search of.

I was now 20 years old and it was my last straw with my codependent relationships after my mother had passed. I didn't know what to do, who to turn to, and I had exhausted my energy of people on earth helping me out. For I learned quickly that they are still figuring things out for themselves. I needed to speak to someone who knew what they were doing, who had all the plans already figured out—shoot, who had me figured out, so much so that they could walk me through. A friend of mine for over 10 years now had been Christian all her life. Throughout high school she would invite me to services and discuss it with me. Of course, I had no desire to really hear it, nor did I come from a home that required me to. I can now say it was the intention of Jesus to knock, plant those seeds, and be there even though I wanted nothing to do with him. I proceeded to give this friend a call because I wanted what I thought would soothe me for the moment: prayer. She proceeded to say to me, "I believe God is calling you." I had no idea what that meant; I just knew that I had nowhere else to go and had tried everything around me, outside me and even in me. I might as well try Jesus.

She led me in a salvation prayer and introduced me to a book from the pastor, called "Purpose Awakening," that I had no idea God would use to teach me as a new believer. The way he taught about purpose through the scriptures revealed to me the very thing I had questions about my entire life. This led me into a time of complete consecration. I sent a message to my friends and family letting them know while I was back at school I would like to focus on God and school. I didn't want any contact from anyone unless I decided to reach out. It was in this place that God began to reveal Himself to me through His word. It showed me myself. It was a mirror to my brokenness, my impurities, my lust, my hurt and my mind. I read things that challenged me; I got mad at God, at myself. I would ask why I didn't know these things all along. It was Romans 8:28 that gave me peace in my frustration: *All things work together for the good of those who love the lord and who are called according to his purpose.* In that I discovered that my existence was not for me but for God, that my life would be used as a representation of His glory. The good, bad, but most certainly the ugly parts were something only He could turn into beauty. Not my self-healing techniques, not astrology and knowing my birth chart, not becoming so spiritual I would get lost in demonic influence more than Holy influence, not sex, masturbation, porn or relationships with men. These things did not give me purpose. Instead, it was the God who knew me before he placed me in my mother's womb (Jeremiah 1:5).

I wish that the moment I said yes, my story would begin in promise. Just as God took the children of Israel through the wilderness after being enslaved in Egypt for years, He needed to do the same for me. I write to tell this because at the time I just thought it was all my fault, when in actuality God had a plan. In 2017, I was now 21 years old, I was baptized, I had given my life completely to Jesus, and though thoughts of masturbation and porn came to mind it was no longer something I bowed to. I had been single for the past eight months, being intentional about dating God. The young man that was trying to get close to me had to go through the trials of fire before getting close. In the months to come God had revealed to the both of us that he would be my husband. Sounds like a happy ending for me, right? I said yes to the Lord, I was learning from the Lord, increasing in my understanding in the walk with Christ, living "right" and not to mention living in LA after being signed to one of the top dance agencies in the city. I would say I had finally had things smoothed and figured out. I didn't realize that God had a completely different plan, that there was more to be exposed and healed in me and that could only be revealed through a certain environment.

In June of 2017, the Lord told me it was time to move back to New York. It was not one of those words I enjoyed obeying but I knew if I didn't, I would have seen a season of homelessness that He did not want me to go through. I had no idea that moving back to my hometown would reveal things that still lay dormant in me since I left that place. It was God's intention to send me back to ensure I was healed from what still lived in me, so that I could walk into promise. My promised husband and I at the time had parted because of distance and immaturity to stay committed to one another during that time. It was the word of the Lord that we would ruin one another if we stayed together, which we began to experience shortly after. This gap between him and me left an emptiness in other places in me that I thought were already dealt with.

In 2018-2019 I would say my life was flipped the complete opposite way. My family and I were evicted from our apartment, which caused a huge divide in my family that I felt spiritually I was in the middle of. While witnessing one side be totally against one party, it was in my nature of Christ to not only intercede in prayer for this matter but leave the 99 for the one, which caused tension toward me for a few years. Not to mention, I was a fresh on fire Christian for Jesus, for which I got mocked a lot by my family, to my face and behind it. It doesn't stop there. I began to see patterns come out of me that I thought had been dismissed because of my yes to Jesus. I started drinking again, smoking again, which in essence led me right back to the door of lust. I thought that I could get to promise without seeing with the correct eyes (God's eyes) the promiscuity that still lived in me. I was raped three times within those two years, entered into a physically and emotionally abusive relationship that God told me not to get into, partied every weekend and sometimes during the week.

It was like this broken girl I thought was healed decided to show out while still serving in ministry, crying in my private time with God daily, reading my Bible, keeping up with the things of God, while feeling like I couldn't even hear God. Throughout the whole time I never gave up on Jesus, never turned my back on the faith; instead, I endured. All the while God was still chasing and having his hand over me. It would seem contradictory for God to even be in something that was so sinful, but I truly believe God saw a heart that wanted to live for Him but was hurting in the process of becoming that. Hebrews 5:8, NLT says, *Even though Jesus was God's son, He learned obedience from the things he suffered.* When I break that down a little deeper, the Holy Spirit revealed to me that Jesus learned to submit to God through sufferings that were brought to him. I would constantly beat myself up about knowing the truth and not obeying it. Coming out of that season, it was through my suffering that I learned to obey. If I didn't come through, I wouldn't understand the value of being submitted to God or the love behind why God asks us to submit and obey. Did I have struggles and temptation in sexual impurity after that? Absolutely, and God was patient with me. In fact, His patience didn't supersede His discipline. I learned things the hard way because of my disobedience. I share this in hopes of being someone's grace. Being promiscuous is something that culture has promoted as feminine power, treating dudes how they treat us, living your best life, YOLO, I'm young these are my years to explore—all deceptive advice from the enemy that tells the young women and men it's ok, when 1 Corinthians 6:18 tells us that it is the only sin that is against our own body, ourselves. I've experienced not living for God in purity, not only in sexual relations, but friendships, actions, my words and thoughts had been detrimental to my identity and purpose.

Is there hope for you? Yes. Why do I say this so confidently? In one of the hardest seasons of my life, where my identity in Christ was being completely slaughtered, God still had a plan. Leading up to 2021, God had worked in me the desire to please Him more than I pleased myself and others. I've seen promotion take place in a year where the world was at a standstill. God called me into purpose for Him, I was promoted twice at my last job within a year, I was making money I had never seen before, I started building my business and ministry that the Lord spoke to me in 2017, and God's ministry of Evangelism began to be worked in me, leading hundreds of people to Jesus during protests, lockdowns and inconvenient times. The Lord restored me and my promised husband to one another, something he spoke in 2017, I am living in now in the year 2021. I am 25 years old and I am proud to say that Jesus is my Lord and Savior, I am a minster of the gospel of Jesus Christ, and my purpose is to live a life that brings glory to God. If that means I'm no longer living my best life to serve my desires, instead living my best life through living out God's desires for me, I would say I have entered into the Promised Land. With much more to explore in this place with God and through Him, I am confident to share my journey of Promiscuity to Purpose.

Dedication

Promiscuity to Promise is a story of a series of events that could have disqualified a young woman from Promise. The encouraging truth that God takes ashes and turns them into beauty is not only for her, but everyone who is willing to surrender their yes to God.

Rachel Titus-Cox is a Program Supervisor for a non-profit mental health and human services organization, that helps support children and families in need of additional services to help them succeed. She has dedicated her career to serving in her community, as well as trying to make a difference in the lives of others. In 2005 Rachel experienced the worst tragedy of her life and nearly gave up. She needed to find a purpose in life that would help her heal and not let this tragedy be in vain. Rachel Joined a grass roots organization, Mother's Against Gun Violence, to help her fulfill this purpose of helping others who had and will experience the same trauma. A while later she became involved in Tamiqa's House, another organization, like Mother's against gun violence, but focused more on helping underserviced youth to receive resources that would help keep them off the streets and help them succeed, she was a sitting Board Member in both organizations.

In 2010 Rachel was nominated and won in her local communities, the Women In Leadership award, presented by the local news organization. Rachel is a mother, wife, and grandmother, who loves spending time with her family and grandchildren. Rachel has faced many adversities in her life but found the strength to endure and overcome and now lives her life with purpose!

THE RESTORATION

Rachel Cox

As I sit here on this curb, it seems as though I am the one who just died. My whole life is replaying before my eyes. I don't feel like I am alive right now; it's like I'm outside of my body looking at the chaos around me. I see a crowd of people whispering, people crying, police running to and fro. This can't be my reality, but as I look to my right and see that blue tarp with just a pair of feet exposed, I realize that this is indeed very real. That is my 22-year-old oldest son under that tarp, and he is dead. Yet I feel like I'm dreaming.

I can't breathe, I can't move, I'm in shock, disbelief and I don't even know what I'm supposed to do at this moment. How can this be happening right now? My whole life just changed, and I don't even know if I want to continue living it. That was on May 21, 2005, 16 years ago, and I couldn't have ever imagined being able to go on after losing my oldest son.

I struggled for months trying to continue living, but every day I woke up from a deep sleep with tears running down my face and an unbearable pain that would hit me from the moment I opened my eyes. I began indulging in activities so foreign to me before now, just to be able to function in a way that seemed somewhat normal to me. I was surviving on Xanax, alcohol, and going out to bars three times a week, just so I could be around people and be distracted from my feelings.

I would come home tipsy and go straight to bed. That was my existence. I didn't think about my family or my youngest son, who had just lost his only sibling and best friend. I had nothing in me to give him or them. I had three beautiful grandchildren left by my son, but I didn't care. The only thing I cared about was not feeling.

This would be my way of life for nearly a year or more, and I really wasn't too concerned if I lived or died at this point. I was losing my faith in everything, and I just wanted my son back. I questioned God. *How could you let this happen? I have served you most of my life, I believed in you and your promises, yet you took my son? Why?* I believed that God had forsaken me, or was punishing me for something I had done. I was angry, hurt, and on a path of self-destruction.

One morning as I lay in my bed, my phone rang. I didn't recognize the number and did not want to answer it. I feared answering my phone since that fateful day, since that was how the day started when I got the call that my son had been shot, but for whatever reason, I felt compelled to take the call. I answered the phone and it was a local DJ and good friend of my late son. He began to tell me of an event coming up and he wanted me to participate in the event. I wasn't sure what role I would play in this event or how going to it would help me. I remember questioning him about what I would have to do. He told me he wanted me to be one of the panelists and to tell Joey's story and by doing this, it would keep my son's memory alive.

I liked the idea of sharing my son's memory with the community, but I'd never done anything like this, and didn't know the first thing about talking to a large group. I didn't think I could do it. I knew I would break down and be unable to get through the first five minutes. I couldn't possibly agree to this and be vulnerable in front of people; they would remember my face and know that I was the lady who cried and couldn't even compose myself at a major event. Yet something inside me was telling me to do it; Joey would want people to know his story. So with some hesitation, I said, "Yes, I'll do it."

On the night of the event, I arrived alone and nervous. I was so scared, and the auditorium was packed. I stood in the back rethinking my participation. I thought to myself, *No one knows me; they wouldn't even know I'm here.* The DJ who invited me was on the stage, so he was too busy to see me, but as I turned to walk out, I was greeted by a woman I had never seen before. She asked me if I needed to find a seat, and without even thinking, I responded, "No, I was asked to speak at the event." *WHY DID YOU JUST SAY THAT, YOU IDIOT?* I thought to myself. *You had a clean escape.*

I told her who I was, and she said, "I was waiting for you." It turned out she was the president of the local Mothers Against Gun Violence (MAGV) organization, and she called me after my son's passing, as she did with all families who had just gone through that trauma. Even though I hadn't met her until that day, I was a little relieved that she was with me. She seemed so reassuring and comforting. She took me to the front of the auditorium and showed me to my seat. Shortly after, I was called up to speak. I closed my eyes, said a quick prayer, and made my way to the front. I began to talk of my beloved son and how losing him had impacted my life, and it seemed as if the words were coming to me faster than I could say them. My voice cracked a few times, but I was able to deliver a compelling presentation without a hitch.

As I was making my way back to my seat after I was done, I felt a tap on my shoulder. I looked down and all I could see was someone handing me a business card, and the woman who was handing it to me said, "Give me a call." So a few days later, I called. She told me she was the organizer for a local event that happened every year, called the "peace rally," and she wondered if I would come and present at that event. I wasn't sure what was happening, and why I was being asked to do all these speaking engagements, but she told me that my story was very inspiring, and people needed to hear it. That was enough for me to accept the offer. What I didn't know prior to accepting was the location of the event. All I knew is that it was on the west side of town, a side of town I try to avoid because that was where the tragedy happened. I would find out too late that this would prove to be the most difficult event of my life to that point.

The day of the event, I called the organizer and asked her where she wanted me to meet her. She told me to meet her at Skiddy Park. "Skiddy Park?" I asked. She said, "Yes, that is where the event is being held." "I can't do that," I told her. "You see, that is the park where my son took his last breath, and the last time I saw him was lying under a tarp at that park. I can't do it; I haven't been there since his death." I thought, *I've been set up. Did she know this was the place that my son died, and if she did, how could she ask me to do such a thing? It's too fresh. I don't want to go there.* These were all the thoughts going through my head. The organizer calmly said to me, "Sweetie, I know this is hard, and if you don't feel you can go through with it, I'll understand." I should've said thank you and bowed out, but I have always been a woman of my word and felt an obligation to adhere to my commitment. I told her, "No, I'll do it." but I needed her right by my side, in case it got too hard. She assured me that she would be right there.

I got to Skiddy Park and my heart dropped. The mobile stage had been set up facing the very spot where my son took his last breath. The corner was still filled with stuffed animals and memorabilia left by people who loved him. I was going into a full-blown panic attack, I couldn't breathe, I was sweating, and I could almost see my heart beating out of my chest. This wasn't going to go well.

The park was filled with people from all over the community, including my youngest son, Joey's children and their mother and many others who came to hear my story. As I looked out in the crowd, I knew I had to keep it together for them. I actually used the location to intensify the ending of my speech. "I want everyone to turn around and look at the corner," I shouted. Everyone turned to the corner, gazing at the teddy bears and balloons. "That is the last place I saw my baby. Don't let another mother have to go through what my family and I are going through," I added. I turned away from the podium and proceeded to exit the stage. The crowd erupted in applause, I stepped off the stage I began to weep. The president of MAGV, was in the audience and ran to embrace me. She comforted me and told me that the community needed my voice, and she wanted me to consider joining MAGV. I really felt a desire to be a part of something, so after a few weeks of contemplation, I did join the organization.

I became a core part of the group, attending every vigil for yet another homicide victim, speaking to and offering condolences to grieving families, giving a lot of news interviews to reporters and participating in several speaking engagements at various venues. I still felt there was something missing. I enjoyed being a part of the organization, but I wanted to do more. One day there was a community barbeque, and I was supposed to speak at the event, but due to circumstances I can't remember, I got there extremely late, and the event was over. I was told by someone that a young girl came to the event because she wanted to talk to me. She had heard me speak at a previous vigil and she was inspired by my story. I was so upset that I had let this young lady down. No one knew her name and no one asked for her contact info, so I could reach out to her. I don't know to this day who she was, but I wanted to know her story and how I could've helped her. I don't know what became of her, but I just pray that she made it through whatever she was going through. It was then that I had somewhat of an epiphany. I wanted to motivate and encourage people that no matter what they were experiencing in life, they could still reach and achieve their dreams. MAGV only focused on one part of people's experiences, but not so much in helping people get to the other side; that's what I wanted to do. I had so much more to share with the world. I am a survivor of so many experiences: family abuse, teen pregnancy, domestic abuse, survival, escape and now the mother of a homicide victim. I needed another platform to tell my stories and possibly help someone going through similar experiences.

I remember coming home from a very emotional vigil for a young man whose situation was very reminiscent of my son's. He was an aspiring rapper, he had a young child and a younger brother, hell-bent on revenge. As I stood in the crowd, the music of the deceased young man playing from someone's car speakers, the younger brother of this young man got more and more emotional. He started screaming how he was going to avenge his brother. The hurt and pain in his voice broke my heart all over again and reminded me of my son, who was still in the same emotional state. I had a conversation with my son telling him not to seek revenge for his brother, because I couldn't bear to lose him too. I begged my son to promise me that he wouldn't seek revenge, because I would have nothing left to live for if I lost him too. I asked the organizer of the vigil if she would ask the young man if I could speak to him. The young man agreed to talk to me. I shared with him that I understood his pain and him wanting to avenge his brother, and how my younger son felt the same way about his brother. I also let him know of my conversation with my son, explaining to him what I told my son it would do to me and the rest of our family if we were to lose him to jail or death. The young man listened intently, his emotions seemed to regulate, and he told me he would let the system handle it, because he didn't want his mother to grieve any further. I'm not sure if he kept his word, as there have been many homicides since, but just knowing that for a split second, I was able to help him see the bigger picture brought a sense of relief that he was not going to go down that path.

As I drove home from the vigil, I began talking to God. I told Him that I need a purpose in life and I want to make my purpose my career and earn a decent living so that I could provide for my family. I wasn't sure which organization to apply to that would allow me to do this work, but I knew God would open the door to the opportunity if one existed for me.

A few months later, I received a phone call from a dear friend. She told me that she was offered a job at a local woman's shelter but she turned it down due to the demands in her life. She said that she gave them my name as a potential candidate and that I would be great for their organization. Sure enough, I got a call from them asking if I was interested in an interview. I was ecstatic. I didn't even know what the job was at the time, but I felt this was all God.

I was offered the job at the organization as a Program Assistant for the domestic violence program for offenders. These clients would be mandated from the court system or various other community agencies to attend a 26-week course. I loved my new job and hit the ground running. Four months later, I would be offered a promotion to be the coordinator for the program, responsible for all aspects: orientations, meeting with judges, the probation department, scheduling classes, and supervising facilitators. I learned a lot while sharing my story of survival. I thought I would retire from this job. However, after two years with the organization, I was in a very bad car accident. I didn't sustain any serious injuries, but I did sprain my back and was out of work for some time. Eventually, the organization filled my position.

I was out of work for over two years due to that accident, and during this time, I got married and took custody of my two-year-old epileptic niece. It was time to go back to the work force, there were no openings at my previous organization, and I struggled to find a job that was anything like the one I had. Again, I went to God in prayer, praying that He would open another door similar to the one He had opened before and that the pay would be equal to or greater than what I was making. I had submitted several resumes to various places and nothing. No phone calls, no offers. Until one day, I received a call from an organization I didn't recognize.

The woman on the other end of the phone asked if I would be willing to come in for a job interview for the Family Engagement Specialist for a county program. I was clueless about this job that I didn't apply for and yet, I accepted the interview. It turns out a friend who was waiting on a grant to offer me a job forwarded my resume to them when the grant fell through and gave me a glowing reference, and I am so thankful he did. I was offered the job working at a local school and from my very first day, I knew this was the job for me. Working with so many children and building so many relationships with families brought great fulfillment to my life. This made me view life differently. I was touching lives and they were touching mine at the same time. God had finally given me a purpose; everything else leading up to that point was preparation for this very moment. I have been with this program for almost nine years and have gone from specialist to supervisor, now supporting and teaching new specialists. The relationships I've gained and the children who have been and some who still are a part of my life have shown me that God is able to restore, if we choose not to give up. I am living proof of that. I believe there is still so much more for me to do, and I will walk through any door He opens. I am a vessel who no longer questions God because I know his plans are always better than ours. He has turned my tragedy and pain into elevation and abundance, and I am in expectation of what He will do next!

Dedication:

I dedicate these words to my Father God, who has carried me through the sand many times in my life and has given me strength to persevere and be a testimony to His awesome power.

Secondly, to my mom and oldest sister, thank you for holding me up during the worst time in my life, for the many tears shared, and the many words of encouragement. I love you so much.

To my son, thank you for being my rock, even when you needed someone to support you. I love you more than words can describe. You are my heart in human form and I hope this brings some encouragement to you as well.

Last, to all the women in the world who are experiencing trauma or are in a situation where you feel trapped and there is no escape, I'm here to tell you, there is help. Look up, and hold on to God's unchanging love, and He will bring you through it and to your destiny.

 **Angela M. Douglas** is a powerful speaker and advocate. She serves as the Co-Executive Director of Vera House in Syracuse, New York. Angela identifies as a victim survivor and serves as the Chair of the Survivors Network. Primary of Angela's work is strategic planning, organizational leadership development and change management to increase capacity and deconstruct social norms that maintain sexual and domestic violence, and oppression, while advocating for systemic change.

Angela serves on the board of directors of New Justice Services, CancerConnects, Alliance of Communities to Transform Syracuse. Living philanthropy, she serves as trustees to the Western and Central New York Health Foundation and Vera House Foundation. Angela has been a consultant for 30 years working to build capacity in nonprofits and serves as Deaconess at Abundant Life Christian Center. She works from the understanding that true success and impact will occur only in the pursuit of healing and wholeness in our souls and relationships.

HORRIBLY BEAUTIFUL

Angela M. Douglas

S*o, after you have* **suffered** *a little while, he will* restore, support, and strengthen you, *and he will place you on a* firm foundation.
1 Peter 5:10, NLT

Beloved while I was very diligent to write to you concerning our common salvation, I found it necessary to write to you exhorting you to **contend earnestly for the faith** *which was once for all delivered to the saints.* Jude 3, NKJV

Suffering never travels alone. Often you can find it accompanied by distress, sorrow, grief and disappointment. They are carried, pulled, stacked and wheeled much like a luxury set of luggage. This is a complete set that needs no ID tag, as they never get separated from their owner, lost in transit, rerouted or left at home. In fact, there are times when additional pieces are needed. Betrayal, loneliness, bitterness and resentment and a nice cosmetic bag of condemnation join the journey, as if we would not be prepared without them.

When in a hurry, we are stuffing and shoving things in each of these pieces of luggage, strapping items in and putting our weight on them to get them zipped and locked, praying and hoping that it meets the weight requirement, and nothing pops out unexpectedly.

Other times, we are thoughtful about organizing our many items with corresponding luggage pieces, examining each, recalling every memory attached and taking inventory of the trauma, victimization and wrongdoings.

Some of us remember the first piece of luggage we ever had. Perhaps the bookbag or lunch pouch for school or our first purse in our favorite color. We learn early in our childhood to carry things. As we get older, however, we stop purging or prioritizing and merely purchase more pieces to help us carry, lug and pull. We are determined to get the best quality luggage, with rollers, combination locks and coordinating colors and patterns. Much like putting lipstick on a pig, we are determined to have our mess, I mean luggage, look good.

In time we become frustrated and angry that we are having to carry so much, organizing, reorganizing, shuffling and reshuffling over and over, working to make room for what we have collected. Over time, we come to the end of ourselves and can no longer carry, pull or lug another piece of luggage. Zippers begin to stick, seams burst and unravel, handles break and wheels fall off. We are exhausted and yet scramble to unload and reload, reassemble, tape and tie up. If only they can last just a bit longer, when I have time, I will downsize and let some things go.

But I don't have time right now. There is too much going on. Children, husband, parents, grandparents, job, church, house, laundry and Saturday hair day all are requiring of me relentlessly. I must keep all of this luggage together and help everyone carry theirs as well.

I find myself getting up early and going to bed late just to ensure that everyone's luggage is packed, prepared and secure for the next day.

Overwhelmed and empty, I recognize that I cannot go another minute without complete collapse. Luggage everywhere. Spilling out and uncontainable. I sit in the middle of my luggage and that of others I have carried, only to see that my soul looks and feels like my luggage and its contents.

I have come to the end of myself. I am overcome by the weight of the luggage. Trauma that I have chosen to carry with me since childhood, collected through each stage of my life, believing that if I kept it all in the luggage, nice and neat, that I would be fine. Never being a burden to anyone else. Every woman in my life has carried, pulled and lugged so much, why should it be different for me?

I have never known anything but to pick up all of the contents and place them back into the luggage. Weary, vulnerable and full of despair, I pray and ask for the strength to reassemble just one more time and that all would fit perfectly into its place. I have not witnessed the healing and deliverance they speak of in the Bible. I just see droves of people who carry, lug and pull their own sets of luggage. I realize that I must not complain but do the same.

My own life has followed this process and pattern for decades, until one incident caused all of my luggage to be irreparable and its contents irrepressible: the sexual assault of my daughter as a high school senior by a man in the ladies' restroom on a local university campus where she worked. This is the very thing that shook my soul and brought me to my knees. Upon hearing and working to remain calm, I was instantly thrown back to my own campus rape and assault on another.

I worked to be attentive to my daughter and her pain. My own flashbacks and suffering kept trying to crowd her out. More and more my luggage and its contents were strewn everywhere. I couldn't turn left nor right. I tried to walk forward but I tripped over everything lying everywhere. My trauma response is numbness and dissociation. I had mastered wonderful external presence, while completely escaping my body and hoping this too shall pass.

It was no longer just my own rape and assault; it was the sexual trauma that I endured as a child and the pain from generational domestic violence that haunted me. The unspoken messages that I had received all of my life that I had packed away and only revisited inconsistently when feeling bad for myself. All of these were trying to steal Momma from my daughter. I was persistent in trying to stay present and realized that I could not. I could not completely hear her. I could not protect her, and I could not heal her. How could I? I was still carrying all of my own luggage.

The deep pain and regret of not downsizing and managing my own luggage now became the focus. I was angry that I could not be what she needed. How could this happen? I did this to her and to me. In the darkness of the days ahead, I had to come to terms that I had not shared much of who I am, nor my luggage, with my children or family. This was not the time to do so. It was not about me. But my luggage was making it impossible for me to be Momma for my daughter and now for our devastated family.

I sat with her. I could not hold her, as the man who tried to destroy her soul had temporarily taken her ability to be physically held and loved. I pushed all the luggage and contents aside and I heard the moaning and painful cries in my baby's soul. With humility and sorrow, I confessed to her that I would not be able to be the best Momma, that I had carried the same pain for far too long. I communicated that I didn't know how to heal, but my love for her was unending and full. It was clear that we both needed to recover and heal. I vowed to myself that I would not allow my lack of work or intended future work to steal any more from her.

I had just started working in full time ministry that January and when my Pastor heard the news, I was called to the office. Not knowing what to expect, I knew I needed to be open to hear, ready to accept and prepared to commit. By the witness of the Holy Spirit, He said this was indeed an attack from the enemy. This bore witness with me and I knew there would be some price to pay for turning my life and time over to the Lord in service to

His body. I just didn't expect or want any harm to come to my family.

I do not remember all of the conversation, as I was fighting to stay present in my body. What I do recall was me confessing all the things that had been done to me since childhood at the hands of many people, which I had never spoken of before. It spewed out like a fountain of sludge. I couldn't turn it off, nor control the speed at which it exited. I expected shame to overcome me, but it didn't. Instead, he suggested that I go to therapy, as that would be best for me and my daughter. For the first time, I felt the burden lift. I knew it was what I must do.

I spent the next five years straight in weekly visits with my therapist, unpacking, inspecting and examining every bit of content from my luggage. My daughter began a similar process in our local rape crisis and domestic violence agency. It is in this place and process that I had permission and was able to experience the deliverance and healing that I have read about in the Bible. I was convinced that I had faith but learned early on that I was never really exercising faith at all. I left the therapist's office angry several days as she questioned my faith. Who was she to question such a thing, when the only reason that I still existed was because of my faith in God? She didn't understand that it had been only God and me my whole life.

I was deluded and unable to grasp the concept of faith in its true sense. Did I trust God? Of course! I am still alive. He saved and kept me all of this time. Indeed, He did, but did I trust Him to heal the suffering, distress, sorrow, grief, disappointment and all the other contents of my luggage? I had been carrying everything in my own strength and praying that I might continue to do so. My faith was wrapped up in God granting me the ability to keep carrying, lugging and pulling all my luggage. I actively committed the sin of self-reliance. Somehow, I never accepted that He didn't want me burdened by the luggage and, in fact, said He would carry it for me. Instead, I was fully surrendered and sold out to being strong and holding it myself.

Pathetic, disillusioned and completely devoid of hope, I chose to settle into the promises of God. While I hadn't seen or experienced healing in this manner and to this degree, I was determined to fight. I would contend for my faith and wrestle with the love of Christ. I learned that being strong was my prison. It is a cultural prison created for women, and particularly women of color, as they are the 'keepers of the soul' in our families. This prison had been passed down to me through the generations. It was my punishment for all the decisions that should have been made differently.

I should have been able to stop and prevent all of the harm done to me. I should have been able to fight back. I should not have been in the library alone. I should have not gone to a party with a friend. I should have made better choices. I shouldn't be letting this still bother me. I should be over all of this by now. I was punishing myself as if I had committed the crimes and was the hand of abuse.

I have spent a tremendous amount of time relearning faith and its application to my life. As the prison doors opened and could now be dismantled, I realized that my challenge was that my distortion of faith was due to it being disconnected from the love of God. It was this inaccurate understanding that required me to carry, lug and pull every bit of luggage without question, despite the weight and burden. The accurate definition of faith that tore down the stronghold and prison that I had made for myself is anchored in this love and compassion from our Most High God. They cannot be disconnected from one another. Ever.

I worked to surrender and let His love repair my soul and become the foundation on which I stand. It was messy and required a large dumpster in which I would purge and burn every item in the luggage that I could. Surrender was painful and at times felt more difficult than managing all of that luggage. Surrender is an act that is continuous. The courage to allow the Great Physician and Healer, Jehovah Rapha to perform His surgery and treatment is not for the faint of heart. In fact, surrender and healing are the most difficult to do. It requires pride, bitterness, envy, resentment and unforgiveness to be laid down permanently.

I wrestled and fought to receive the love of God and stand in faith as His daughter. Not only was my understanding of faith distorted, but so was my understanding of His love. I could not fathom it. I didn't know how to make sense of it. How did I earn it? I wanted to know how to repay it. There must be an exchange, just like every person in my life was expecting something in return. My body must be the payment, as it is the thing that has been taken over and over, even that of my daughter.

It finally became clear that in my complete surrender and receiving of His love, I would be healed, delivered and set free, and the only thing I needed to do was trust Him to do it. FAITH. Trusting our Father to do what He always intended. My repayment to Him is my enduring trust in Him. *And without faith it is impossible to please him, for whoever would draw near to God must believe that he exists and that he rewards those who seek him.* Hebrews 11:6, ESV

This was a huge challenge to overcome, recognizing that I am loved and wanted, not just needed. That it is not my performance of faith, but my sincere and earnest trust that He is who He says He is. This was the beginning of being set free. I no longer had to perfectly keep everything together, which I was not doing and was completely unable to do. It's amazing the narratives that we feed ourselves in order to keep our lives going. I laid them all down and got comfortable with me.

I remember eighteen months of crying in the shower asking God where I was. I could not locate myself. I would wait for the hot water to fog up the shower doors and I would write questions to God with my fingers like a schoolgirl, praying that He would answer. I would continue to cry out in pain and fully exposed in every sense. I would clean up and as my act of faith say, "Lord, I don't know where I am, but I know You do. I am not lost in You." I would then continue on the journey to healing.

As the unpacking continued, I began to find other contents that, if not corrected, would hinder the full healing and deliverance that the Lord intended for me. Unforgiveness is brutal. We can read about it and are able to experience people in our lives who are utterly destroyed, because they are unable to forgive. This was not the challenge for me. Somehow, since I was a small girl, I have forgiven everyone who had harmed me. I always had the vision of Christ on the cross asking His Father to forgive those who persecuted him. I have always been moved by that and recognized that when people are harmed and broken, much like myself, they hurt others. This forgiveness seemed simple.

However, there was one who I could not forgive that nearly killed me. It strangled me, kidnapped me and held me hostage for years. I could not forgive myself. My mind and soul couldn't let go. They needed someone to blame. They needed to hold someone responsible and accountable. What I eventually learned is that I could control myself, but not others. It was far easier to continue to punish, put down and demonize myself. I couldn't let go of all of the "should haves." I needed them and they had teamed up with condemnation to keep me in my lane. They had become my identity of failure and weakness.

One evening while washing dishes my teenage son and I were talking about the day and he said, "Mom, can I ask you a question?" I replied, "Of course." He said, "You used to be bold! What happened?" I immediately became defensive and stated, "I am bold." Then I felt the Holy Spirit and knew he was speaking truth.

I was no longer bold or any of who I had intended or desired to be. I then asked him to explain, and he shared much insight with me. He spoke of and described the boldness that he remembered as a child. He told me that it had been gone for quite some time and that God needed me to have it back. I sought the Lord about my boldness and discovered that if I cannot forgive even myself then I cannot become who He created me to fully be. *Be kind to one another, tenderhearted, forgiving one another, as God in Christ forgave you.* Ephesians 4:32, ESV. I had never been kind, loving or forgiving to myself. This, too, became another leap into freedom as I began practicing forgiveness with myself.

This luggage was mine to own, unpack and purge. Holding up and examining the suffering, pain, trauma and despair gave me the opportunity to recognize what was not mine and to discard it.

I forgave myself for burdening and harming me in hopes of protecting everyone else. I reclaimed my body, soul, voice and dreams without apology. I have less luggage now. I have kept the process of purging and healing. I am determined to be whole and healthy and trusting God to do it in me.

Life is hard. It comes with much to make sense of and journey through. We don't have to carry, lug and pull all of the luggage with us. The Lord never intended us to. Consider surrendering it to Him and opening yourself up to a new beginning. He heals and restores. He provides strength in our weakness and gives us joy. I pray that as you have read this chapter, the Holy Spirit has highlighted pieces of your luggage. He desires you to turn them over to Him. You will never regret it. It is the most wonderful and horribly beautiful surrender that we can make. It is our step toward transformation.

Dedication

Horribly Beautiful is dedicated to ALL of the women in my life who have persisted for liberation, love, joy, and peace, realizing that the luggage they have been carrying, lugging, and pulling has sabotaged them. We are worthy and deserve the life that God has promised. I invite every woman to examine and purge our luggage so that our children and grandchildren can secure the life we intend them to have. To my daughters, Alivia, Alandra, Alasia, and Trinity, your destinies are secure in Christ! Be bold. Abide in the love of God and contend for the FAITH.

"She stood in the storm
and when the wind did
not blow her way, she
adjusted her sails."

Elizabeth Edwards

Stephanie Rena' Williams is a Bestselling author, poet, and entrepreneur. She is an ordained Evangelist. Stephanie is the CEO of 180 Turn In, a signature fragrance designer, former rape crisis advocate, Who's Who 2004-2006 recipient, certified life coach, and professional makeup artist. Stephanie is a woman of influence, encouragement, and supporter of those whom God placed in her path. Stephanie has a passion for the lost, and heartbroken, from which she has also overcome those same issues and her life.

Stephanie's experiences in her life include physical abuse, rape, rejection, low self-esteem, depression, fear, anxiety, worthlessness and a suicide attempt. Stephanie is graced by God to love others without judgement with the love of Christ. She is determined to spread the good news so that many are delivered and set free. Stephanie has strived, persevered, and kept her faith, which allowed her to become the strong resilient woman she is today. Stephanie is a mother of 3, and grandmother of 5. Stephanie currently resides in the beautiful city of Savannah, Georgia.

BEHIND MY MANY FACES (I SURVIVED, I PERSEVERED, I KEPT THE FAITH)

Stephanie R. Williams

I often wonder what people see when they look at me, all made up, looking as if I have it all together. I pondered with this repeatedly throughout my life as a child, young adult, and most of my adult life. No one could discern what was behind the selfies, the hugs, smiles, laughter, the many different expressions on my face.

An outgoing, vibrant, silly, humble caring woman—who would think? Who could have known? I was being strong for everyone, but who was strong for me? That question, I truly believe all of us have asked or have thought about asking.

I laughed, I smiled; no one could discern the brokenness, the pain, the emotional rollercoaster ride. I kept on praying, I kept on praising, I kept pressing. Some thought it was to be seen; however, they never knew, they said I was crazy...I never said a word, not wanting to be judged even more.

I laughed, I smiled, I had suicidal thoughts at the age of six. I felt unworthy, ashamed, depressed, defeated, didn't trust not a soul. The struggles were real. I kept repeating that *all things work together for good to them that love God, to them who are called according to his purpose.* Romans 8:28, KJV. I would tell myself to handle it, each test, every trial, like a good soldier.

I would cry, wondering what these people see when they look at me. I was messed up, but not realizing how messed up I really was. How did I allow myself to become so dysfunctional? I experienced loneliness, even while married. No one discerned that cry for help, that silent anger, the abuse, yet I laughed and I smiled.

I suffered from low self-esteem, being so tall, and my weight, for 34 years to be exact. I heard what was said. They said I was stuck up, knowing I feared standing up in front of large audiences. No one knew of the emptiness that I felt inside. "BONDAGE"—I needed to be free.

I drank, along with taking meds, not wanting to deal with the drama, especially in front of my kids. I praised, I worshipped, I shouted to keep from losing my mind. They thought I wanted to be seen. Not at all, that was the farthest thing from my mind. No one could imagine what I felt, what was in my spirit. I was in deep bondage; Stephanie was STUCK. Imprisoned in my mind.

I thought to take my life as a child, and as an adult. I continued to pray and praise, but thinking to myself, *Who truly cares about me?* I was tired of being judged by the cosmetics on my face, especially by other believers. They had no idea; that was my little secret, the silent anger, depression, aggravation. I laughed, I smiled, holding on to God's unchanging hands.

I kept waiting on the Lord, I kept staying encouraged, the Lord continued to strengthen my heart. That hole in my Spirit only God could fill. I cried day in and day out for someone to understand and not judge, wanting someone to love me, genuinely love me with the love of Jesus Christ.

> *Many are the afflictions of the righteous; but the Lord delivereth him out of them all.* Psalm 34:19, KJV

I received several negative diagnoses, I laughed, I smiled, yet no one knew my faith walk was being challenged. I had children to provide for, in turn experiencing near death. I struggled mentally; I kept many things to myself. Why? Glad you asked. You see, I have always been the strong one, no matter what situation occurred. I kept laughing, I kept smiling, I kept pressing.

I dealt with liver disease, kidney problems, several back procedures, nerve damage, lost mobility in one leg, along with other negative reports from the doctors. I kept smiling, I kept laughing, I kept praising, worshipping, praying, shouting, believing Jehovah Rafa, my healer. I knew this was a God thing; this was out of my control—no doubt about that. I continued with total assurance, by faith, knowing that I was already healed. I purposed to praise my way out. It wasn't about me, this test...It was for those who needed the faith to know that God will heal the sick, that they shall recover.

Being an outgoing individual, I loved on everyone I met, while purposing to be more loving and kinder every day of my life. It was as if the more I loved the more I became rejected. I kept laughing, I kept smiling, no one could discern. Why? We are supposed to be our brother's keeper.

No one knew of the emptiness, the anxiety, the loneliness, when my rose and my angel transitioned. Coping with these deaths, my relationship with the Lord kept me from a deep depression. I was hurting so badly. My Grammy was my best friend. Her love was endless; no matter how many mistakes I made she loved me. Now she was gone.

I would praise God so much that I would forget about everything that I was bound by. If you don't know my story, you must not judge my praise.

Some things were self-inflicted. The Bible reminded me that if I make my bed in hell, God is there. I realized that I wasn't perfect; none of us are. I realized that people are who they are. I realized

I couldn't make people love me, no matter how loving and kind I was. I am an original; God placed a beautiful spirit inside me, a spirit that loves, encourages, and influences. A supportive woman who loves Christ, who loves people, who is anxious for nothing, yet patiently waiting on the Lord to do that which He desires in my life. He, the Lord our God, gets the glory.

I began to practice being silent, as the Holy Spirit worked on me.

Calming that Spirit of defense, I became sedated by the Holy Spirit's comfort; He became my defense. God healed me from the core of my heart. I can honestly say when tests arise, I take it in differently. No longer am I concerned about the thoughts of others, nor do I fear what is to come in my life. I am one of God's beautiful creations.

I kept silent, I stayed quiet, I smiled, I laughed, during the times my character was being tainted. No one spoke up for me. I was disliked and rejected for numerous reasons. I honestly didn't understand. I know now a Spirit is just a Spirit, good, bad or ugly. I choose to fight evil with good. I had to love me, regardless of how other people treated me...that had me bound for years. I allowed people to treat me badly. I only wanted to be loved and cared about.

I am now free and delivered. I no longer worry about the opinions of others that had put me in that "BONDAGE." I had to understand that my life belonged to the almighty God, I understood that if God could trust me with trouble, He is magnificent enough, God enough, to bring me through.

My afflictions were many; however, the Lord delivered me out of them. I refuse to be defeated. I look forward to helping others and winning souls for the kingdom of God. To trust is an enormous factor in my life when it comes to others, due to the betrayal and rejection. I had to learn to love Stephanie in the midst of it all, not putting others' feelings before my own. I almost destroyed myself. I learned to love me over all things, to lean and depend on my heavenly father. The Holy Spirit was and still is my comforter. I had to trust the Lord and lean not unto my own understanding. The Lord has always been with me, faithful to me.

The Bible says, *After you have suffered a little while, the God of all Grace, who has called you to his eternal glory in Christ will himself, restore, confirm, strengthen, and establish you.* 1 Peter 5:10, ESV.

But he knows the way that I take for when he has tried me, I shall come out as pure gold. Job 23:10, NIV. A major part of my deliverance and my recovery was prayer, spending time with the Holy Spirit, who taught me some life lessons. I was shown myself first. I never said I was perfect. We all have a past, a future, and a present.

Through all the hurt, disappointments, pain, emotional, physical, and verbal abuse, sexual assault, the loss of loved ones, the rejection, judgment, and the health issues, I am still here, determined to repent, love, forgive, let go and live. We must forgive those who hurt us and use us, those we allowed to manipulate us.

I laughed, I smiled, I kept on praising, kept on shouting, kept on praying, kept on worshipping. I continued pressing. I am like the pine tree; I will bend but never break. The Bible declares by the blood of the Lamb, and by the word of thy testimony. Trusting God during it all, throughout the years, I am so grateful for the Lord's love and kindness toward me. I am nothing without Him, our Lord and Savior, sovereign amazing father, my joy, my peace, my comforter, faithful, righteous, redeemer, mind regulator, restorer, resurrector, majestic in all His splendor.

The joyful, laughing, kind, confident, bold, encouraging, loving, grateful woman of God, He has purposed me for such a time as this. I purpose to give hope to the downcast head, to love those others reject with the Love of Jesus Christ. I will continue to let my light shine bright for the kingdom of God. I shall continue to speak of His greatness, His wondrous acts, His love that never fails.

I am a survivor, I am victorious, I am an overcomer. I will freely in my Spirit continue to laugh, to smile, pray, praise, shout without explanation. I am FREE! I survived, I persevered, I kept the faith. I am a resilient woman behind my many faces.

Dedication

I dedicate my chapter to the women of this world who have experienced various traumas in their lives: the abuse, being misunderstood, rejection, hopelessness, loneliness, depression, grief, divorce, to name a few. Trust that there is life after tragedy and trauma. God is a keeper; your journey will help another sister come out of the pits of despair, out of bondage. YOU are not alone. God heals the brokenhearted. Look at me. Resilient!

"I am not what happened
to me. I am what I choose
to become."

Unknown

Mrs. Pamela Jean Williams of Clay, NY, is married and a mother. She is a 15-year survivor of stage 4 colon cancer and a licensed Evangelist for over 25 years. Pamela is the owner, designer and seamstress of K'HARISMA DESIGNS. She is a mentor to youth and women that have been abused and rejected. Pamela uses her wisdom and ministering skills to help them to get up and begin to thrive in life. She encourages young and older women of how to love themselves. Most importantly, she wants them to know that they are loved by God. Pamela hosts prayer sessions and small gatherings in her home for women and private one-on-one sessions, as well. Through evangelism, she has hosted events to bring men and women to Christ. They've been healed from addictions, abuse and more.

Pamela enjoys hosting events like "Dining with the King", cancer benefits/fundraisers, and fashion shows to help people who face financial crises and bring healing to the hearts and bodies of those who attend. Pamela volunteers and serves at Abundant Life Christian Center in East Syracuse, NY. Her mission is to see and help as many people find their way to Jesus. She loves to make women feel beautiful about themselves and to tell everyone she meets that Jesus loves them. She enjoys family time with her loving husband, children and grandchildren. Pamela especially enjoys traveling with her husband Stephen D. Williams Sr. They've been married 28 years strong.

3 MISTERS, BUT 1 HIM

Pamela J. Williams

My life was not filled with perfection and fairytale endings. I didn't end up with Prince Charming; however, by the end of this chapter you will see that I married "Him."

Let me take you on a journey that I experienced with my Misters and Him. Back in the early 1970s, I was a junior in high school. Young, pretty, creative, but also impressionable and a little naïve. I was the eldest daughter in a large family. I had to help take care of my younger siblings at times, while my newly single mother worked long hours to be sure we had everything we needed.

While in high school, I was focused on my studies, and I enjoyed sewing clothes. But this guy Mr. M caught my eye. He was so fine. I didn't know he was watching me the whole time. We started dating and, though we were young, we fell in love. You couldn't tell me anything. I thought this was it for me. Mr. M was all the man that I had hoped for. I'm talking career goals, money and even a car. When you're that young, that is a winner. I was so happy. It wasn't long into our relationship that we found out that I was pregnant with our first child. I was 17 and he was 19. We were happy but nervous all at the same time. Nine months later she was born. I was a new mother, and I had my own family now.

It was Christmas Eve at his parent's house, in front of his family, when he proposed to me. Of course, I said yes. All along, Mr. M was planning to go into the Armed Forces. He also was working at a well-known car factory in the city we lived in. I was still living with my mother, and it was about two years later when we got married.

On our honeymoon we conceived our second child, a baby boy. While Mr. M was away serving in the military, I was trying to thrive in college while working at a daycare and raising our children. It was difficult trying to find a place to live and manage everything as a wife and mother. I really needed help, especially financially. So I applied for public assistance and food stamps. I honestly did the best that I knew how. My life wasn't getting easier, at that time, as a young mother. My husband was gone serving our country and I was getting very little to support me and our two children. Though the struggle was real, I had to push through it to get an apartment and furnish it all on my own. I had no help from Mr. M.

We waited on him to finally come home from the military for good. It was my goal to make sure everything was perfect and set up so we could grow as a family. I was so happy when he first arrived home from the military. However, things took a turn for the worse quickly. Mr. M was not even home two weeks and was cheating on me with other women. How did we get here? I wondered. His cheating hurt me deeply. Then he went on to abandon me and the kids by moving into his father's house. What in the world was happening? I asked myself. Did I miss the memo or something? I was devastated and an emotional wreck.

We didn't see Mr. M for days at a time. I remember crying while I walked the kids to his father's house to talk. There he was, washing his truck as if he didn't see us standing there. I asked him, "Why, why would you do this to us?" He stood there and couldn't bring himself to explain to me at the time, because he had another girl hiding upstairs. I couldn't believe it. He didn't even acknowledge us. I found out later it was someone I knew. I became numb in my body and still had no explanation as to why he chose to leave us.

While still in college, working and trying to get past my hurt, I just dropped the ball on being his "good girl" because it was no longer good for me. Instead, I went out partying with friends and meeting new people. Basically, I was living my life the way I wanted to. It was a rollercoaster ride. Soon that ride came to a stop. When I found out that girl that was hidden upstairs was pregnant by my husband, that's when I decided to go through with a divorce. I tried to move on. It was hard for me. I was humiliated, felt trapped, manipulated, rejected and abandoned, all at the same time. That's when I started going out again even more, trying to cope with the devastation of it all. I was doing me and enjoying myself at parties with friends from college. I had to get Mr. M out of my head and heart.

While I was twirling and doing the latest dance moves on the dance floor, there was another Mister, in a club full of people: Mr. G., a New York City man. He wasn't like the guys I knew from the city where I resided. He was fun; he had it going on, if you know what I mean. Mr. G was in college for communications in radio/television. Oh my God, he truly had the voice for it. He was a nice guy with all the right things I needed and wanted to hear at that time.

We started dating and going out. He was a DJ at the local skating rink. My children and I were having a great time with him. It felt like what was missing came back. Family. That's it, it felt like family again. I wanted to keep hope that a happy family could still happen for me. Time went on and Mr. G wanted more than just dating. He wanted me to meet his family back in New York City. You know what that means when a man brings you to meet his family. I was so thrilled. That was the first time in a long time I was shown by a man that he really cared about me and my kids.

We were still courting for a year, and he asked me to move to New York City with him. So that is just what the kids and I did. Before moving to NYC we lived in Atlanta for a few months. We got engaged there and he decided to go back to New York City to work, and I would work in Upstate NY until we got married. Within a year, we planned to have our wedding and get married in New York City. That was our plan, and that's just what we did.

The first couple of years of our marriage I worked at a department store, sewed clothes and styled hair. I worked around the clock to support my family. This was my life then. It was a good life, with fancy cars, furs, diamonds, designer clothes and fine dining. Then there was shift in my life. I desired more than "stuff." Instead, I wanted a real relationship with God. I started going to Monday night prayer and Bible study regularly. I knew in my heart that God was changing me and my kids. All the while, Mr. G was changing too. And right before my eyes, this man was acting like he wanted to be single again and wasn't being the husband who committed to me.

I should've been familiar with this. He started lying to me, manipulating me, mentally abusing me and you guessed it, he was cheating on me too. How was I so blind? But I couldn't leave him because I was so embarrassed, so I just dealt with it. I almost felt like I had to stay to prove it was going to work out. I was stronger than the last marriage. I wasn't going to run. I was going to stay. All the while, when I was working Mr. G was on the phone with other women, flirting and having inappropriate conversations with other women. There was one time he was doing just that and had no clue my daughter was in her room and could hear his conversations. What she heard really hurt my daughter's feelings. So she called upstate to my mother and told her what Mr. G was doing.

As time went on, I had to send my kids back upstate to be with their grandmother, so I could deal with the situation on my own. To be honest, I didn't know what I was really going to do. I just knew I had to do something. By the time I went to him in hopes that we would reconcile, I was hit with hard reality that it was too late. Here we go again, another woman this time. She actually came inside the house to meet my husband while we were in another room talking. Right there in front of me at my mother in-law's house, she repeated what he told her when I wasn't there. "He doesn't want you. He said he was leaving you for me!" I was so torn apart. Here I was in front of my husband, his family and the other woman being humiliated. As I was looking at him, hoping that he would explain, he stood there and said absolutely nothing.

I had to get out of that house. Thank God for my friend. She let me stay at her house until I could put my life back together. I was still working and sending money to my mother to take care of the children, while I went through the worst part of my life. Months went by and I was doing what I had to do. On the outside I looked beautiful and strong. I was dressed well and had my own money. But on the inside my life was a mess. I couldn't pretend to be ok anymore, so I prayed and cried out to God. It was at that moment I needed Him to show me the way out and get away from it all. What else could I do? All I had at that time was mustard seed faith. Boy, I needed peace like never before.

Weeks later, my mom called me and told me to come home. I didn't want to go back home. I was healing and didn't want to face my family and people who knew me back upstate. Well, God had other plans for Pamela Jean. I got a call that Mr. Steve was on the way. My mother got all in my business. She sent my "Him," a childhood friend for over 25 years, Mr. Steve, to come get me and bring me back home. Mommy knew I wouldn't come on my own because I just didn't want to at that time.

I finally agreed to leave NYC, but before Mr. Steve came to get me, I was at my sister in-law's house making sure this was what I really wanted to do. Guess what the devil tried to do? Mr. G came to see me. There I was at my sister in-law's house, face to face with Mr. G again. She left us in the house to talk it out. He was apologizing to me and saying to please give him another chance. He told me he was sorry and to come back home. I didn't know what to say, but the word "yes" flew out of my mouth.

My emotions were playing with me, and I almost fell for his charm. I had to snap out of it and shake myself loose. What was I doing? I decided in that moment that this was the end. I was leaving. I made up my mind. I had already made arrangements to get out of New York City. Mr. G didn't know my friend Mr. Steve was on the way to get me. I didn't need to think about it again. I didn't need to work out anything. This was the way of escape for me. A broken marriage full of infidelity, lies, and pain wasn't God's best for me, and I came to grips with that.

The whole time I had no idea how ill my mom was back in Upstate NY with my kids. That was one of the two reasons she needed me to get home. God had my full attention. He allowed me to see the truth unfold before matters got way out of control. I knew His hand was on me, but I was so blinded by Mr. G and how I thought staying was the right thing to do for a moment. I almost stayed in that mess of a marriage that I was in. Thank God for Mr. Steve. If he didn't get me out of there when he did, if he didn't "find" me when he did, I don't know where I would be right now. You see, God used Mr. Steve. He really saved my life from a cheating and abusive husband. He looked me in my eyes and told me he would take care of me and my children.

I took a deep breath. It was different this time. It was different because he was my friend; he knew me for real. I knew to trust his words. That's when I decided to trust God with my whole heart for the first time and I NEVER looked back.

The hours in the car ride back to Upstate NY were long. It seemed like time stood still. I was constantly reminded that another failed marriage happened. The process of healing was so painful. I was so hurt and afraid. This time I had two teenage children looking at me. What was I going to do? I wondered. You see, they were hurt too. At that point in my life, I realized how important it was to ask GOD to show me the way. I did not want to make another bad choice; I couldn't be blindsided again by another man.

When I arrived home my mom was waiting on me. She stood there and looked at me. "It's going to be all right, Pam. God got you, baby." I was trying to be strong because I knew she was ill, but the tears fell. My mother could see what was going on and she had already prepared Mr. Steve with what was to come and how to handle me. I spent all my time with the kids, my mother, and Mr. Steve over the next few weeks.

I'll never forget one evening when it was time to go to bed. I was walking behind my mother to the bathroom. She fell on her knees, and I couldn't get her up. My son's stepbrother called the ambulance for us. The ride to the hospital was scary. I had so much fear and numbness in my body. I was quiet and she kept saying to me, "I'm ok. You'll be all right. Come on now, don't worry about me, Pam." We got her into a room at the hospital. She was fine at first and then it happened.

All of a sudden, I heard them call code blue. My heart dropped as the doctors and nurses ran into her room to save her, but it was too late. She was gone; the Matriarch, the Queen of our family left this world. I didn't know what to do being there by myself and couldn't find my siblings right away to come up to the hospital. I was able to contact my aunt and uncle. They came up and then my siblings arrived later. I couldn't believe it; she was gone.

How was I going to recover from that loss? Two failed marriages and now my mother was gone. What was happening? How much more could I take? I had to pull on my faith now more than ever.

Mr. Steve saw my pain. He was such a great shoulder to lean on. I remember he said to me again, "Pam, you don't ever have to worry about anything ever again. I got you and the children. I promise you. We will be a family."

It seemed so fast. He moved us into a house and told me he wanted to marry me. I didn't know he had already asked my father and even my mother, before she died, for my hand in marriage. I was so nervous. Who gets married three times within a 15-year time span? Was I crazy? Was this wrong? Should I wait longer? No, I realized that I wasn't desperate for love this time, and I didn't need a man to take care of me. I needed the peace of God so I could build a life the way it was always supposed to be. I felt a relief; I felt revived and renewed in my mind and heart. This was God speaking and moving in all of our lives. This was marriage #3, and I was not gonna go through another heartbreak or divorce ever again.

I had to get real honest, real fast. This man heard the heart of my mother, and he was my brother's best friend. He drove hours and helped me pack up my life in NYC. He instantly loved my children as if they were his own. This was all happening for my good.

I'm so grateful to have him in my life today. I'm proud to be "Mrs. Steve." One year of courtship/engagement, 28 years of marriage and 50-plus years of friendship.

Here's the thing: Pamela had to learn to love herself first. I had to forgive myself and forgive those other two "Misters." I had to let go of the shame and guilt. It was not my fault that I trusted and loved them. I do not know why I had to go through all that then, but I know now. Let this story, as rocky and painful as it was for me, teach others a lesson. God can allow things to happen just to get your attention. His perfect will is what you should strive for, and nothing less. I want women and men to know there's life after heartbreak. You can love and trust again. There's someone out there who will love you and your children. You can live in peace. You can learn through my painful experience. Do not hold on to grudges. Please forgive them and yourself too.

My prayer for you, the reader, is the scripture 2 Corinthians 4:16-18, NIV:

Therefore we do not lose heart. Though outwardly we are wasting away, yet inwardly we are being renewed day by day. For our light and momentary troubles are achieving for us an eternal glory that far outweighs them all. So we fix our eyes not on what is seen, but on what is unseen, since what is seen is temporary, but what is unseen is eternal.

By the way, my mother told me Mr. Steve was "Him."

Dedication

I dedicate my chapter to my husband Stephen D. Williams Sr., my beautiful children Melissa and Melvin Jr. and my mother Vider "Maggie" Patterson. Keep resting in the Lord, Mom!

Patasha Burston is a 48-year young Kingdom Enterpriser and entrepreneur born and raised in Philadelphia, Pa. Patasha is recognized as a voice of hope for those that have been misunderstood, abused and discarded by the church and the world. Since March 2019, during the Covid-19 pandemic, Patasha built several businesses and life-changing ministries: RU'AACH, Kairos Kingdom Kreations, OverComer's University and Women's ICU. Patasha is a survivor of domestic violence, child molestation, addiction and prostitution. She has also overcome what many are too afraid to discuss and that is mental and emotional abuse at the hands of church leaders. Some call it "CHURCH HURT" but Patasha calls it "SPIRITUAL RAPE."

Though Patasha has been through much in her life, she still chooses to hold on to the one promise God has made to her in Joel 2:21, "I will repay you for the years the locusts have eaten—the canker worm, the caterpillar and the palmer worm, my great army that I sent among you. You will have plenty to eat, until you are full, and you will praise the name of the LORD your God, who has worked wonders for you; never again will my people be shamed."

FREEDOM LOOKS GOOD ON ME: THE DAY I DECAPITATED JEZEBEL

Patasha Burston

What you are about to read may or may not be a part of your story, but my prayer is that whoever sets their eyes upon this chapter of this life-changing book will receive healing, deliverance and ultimately obtain their right to be free. I decree in the name of Jesus that after reading this chapter, the chains of bondage will be broken off your life and the demonic muzzle will be removed from your mouth. I decree that your mind will be renewed and transformed and a spirit of supernatural boldness will come upon you in Jesus name. Get ready, brace yourself because this chapter has been strategically pulled together by the HOLY SPIRIT and will expose the enemy's tactics to keep God's sons and daughters bound.

Revelations 2:20-23, TPT: *But I have this against you: you are forgiving that woman Jezebel, who calls herself a prophetess and is seducing my loving servants. She is teaching that it is permissible to indulge in sexual immorality and to eat food sacrificed to idols. I have waited for her to repent from her vile immorality, but she willingly refuses to do so. Now I will lay her low with terrible distress along with all her adulterous partners if they do not repent. And I will strike down her followers with a deadly plague. Then all the congregations will realize that I am the one who thoroughly searches the most secret thought and the innermost being. I will give to each one what their works deserve.*

It took over 20 years but I'm finally becoming the woman God has called me to be and I must say, "FREEDOM LOOKS GOOD ON ME!" Well, this chapter is about something many like to call CHURCH HURT but after having a candid conversation with the Lord one day while I was in complete distress concerning the ministry I was under at the time, God began revealing to me that He no longer wanted to hear me use the phrase "CHURCH HURT." The Lord began explaining to me that all I had experienced had nothing to do with the church, but it had everything to do with the spirits that were in operation through those that I chose to lead me. The Lord said to me, "Patasha, what you have been experiencing all these years is called SPIRITUAL RAPE and it is carried out by the spirit of Jezebel!" Jezebel is a spirit that controls, manipulates, intimidates, seduces, suppresses, oppresses and eventually causes both men and women within a ministry to practice immorality and idolatry. The whole purpose of this spirit is to ensure that the people of God do not maximize their potential in God and what He has called them to become.

I remember being introduced to the church as a young girl and I fell in love with the church, not realizing years down the line, I would come to hate it and despise God. Yes, there was a period in my life that I literally hated everything about the church and God, and I walked away from them both for over a year.

COGIC, Church of God in Christ was the first denomination I was introduced to. I really did not have a choice but to go to church because the parochial school I attended at the time required that

I belong to a church or a parish. Isn't that something? In order to attend a Catholic school, I had to belong to a church! In hindsight, this was all a part of God's master plan to draw me unto Himself and to begin the journey that would lead to my destiny and purpose.

Going to church every Sunday and even several days during the week for prayer became almost, if I might say so, an addiction. I became so addicted to belonging to something that allowed me the opportunity to escape the constant abuse I endured at home. Church became my fix, my hit, until one day, it became my worst nightmare, worse than what I was experiencing at home.

If you're paying attention, I didn't say I became addicted to God, so what was I addicted to? All the theatrics. I became addicted to the whooping and hollering from the preachers, shouting and doing the church shuffle all over the place. You know that dance that everybody in the church does every time that certain beat is played on the drums and keyboard. I became addicted to listening to people scream out in the middle of a sermon, partaking in all the latest, hottest gossip and those big Sunday chicken dinners after service.

To this very day, I could not tell you one sermon that was preached. All I know is, I knew what to expect every single Sunday I showed up and the very people I trusted to take care of my soul and help me heal the shattered pieces of my heart became the very ones who tried to finish the job the enemy started. Yes, I said it. Listen, if you are reading this and you feel I am saying things I shouldn't say, skip this chapter and move on because I told you in the beginning, FREEDOM LOOKS GOOD ON ME and I will not apologize for being completely and totally transparent.

Who the Son sets free is free indeed. John 8:36, KJV

The day my life changed for the worse started with a kiss. It was the kiss that sent my life into a never-ending downhill spiral. The kiss…I have played it over and over again in my mind, trying to figure out how and why. He was the co-pastor. He was married. I was only

15 years old. He was old, half- bald, unattractive, and on that day, he became the door that opened the floodgates of hell over my life.

As if I did not have enough on my plate to deal with—I was already dealing with the abuse at home. I was already struggling with my sexuality. I was already dealing with my father leaving me behind and entrusting me into the hands of a woman who mentally, emotionally and physically abused me. I was already contemplating suicide almost on a regular basis. I was already dipping into witchcraft. I was already consumed by low self-esteem, low self-worth, depression, anxiety and stress. I was already diving into the abyss of pornography and masturbation and now this? Why would God allow all of this to happen to me? What could I have possibly done to make this man think it was ok for him to do such a thing? To make matters worse, I thought I was doing the right thing by going to the mother of the church and letting her know what happened, but her only response was a smirk on her face and blatantly telling me that the co-pastor did not mean to do it and not to tell anyone else. When this woman diminished what I said to her and gave this man an excuse, I didn't know it then, but I found out that was only the beginning of my suffering for years to come.

From that point forward, I endured so much heartache and torment at the hands of several leaders. There were days that I felt like there was a deliberate target on my back and at any moment, I would be assassinated. I had no idea that the reason I was being targeted was because I had a prophetic call on my life and the enemy knew it. As God began developing me, Jezebel showed up on the scene. I had no idea that I was a threat to the enemy, but I found out that leaders saw in me what I did not see in myself.

The attack on my life continued and it escalated to leaders having secret conversations about me and spreading vicious rumors about me that hurt me to the core of my being. Once God started using me, leaders would immediately come against me. There was no support when I would minister, or someone would try to disrupt my spirit by speaking something to me that would throw me off. I never would retaliate but my heart would sink. If that wasn't enough, men in the church would try to seduce me and express their sexual desires for me. To some of you, that may not seem like a big deal but when the man is married to your leader, it is a very big deal. I've had female leaders accuse me of misinterpreting the situation and of course, I ended up leaving that ministry. If that was not enough, I encountered leaders who tried to control me by telling me that I should not be listening to any other voice but theirs, therefore visiting other ministries was not welcomed. I have experienced being accused of stealing, pulling people out of the church and starting my own ministry. I have experienced being shunned, excommunicated, called a witch and have even had a leader pray against my life and I ended up literally on my death bed.

Jeremiah 1:5-10, MSG says, *Before I shaped you in the womb, I knew all about you. Before you saw the light of day, I had holy plans for you: A prophet to the nations—that's what I had in mind for you." But I said, "Hold it, Master God! Look at me. I don't know anything. I'm only a boy!" God told me, "Don't say, 'I'm only a boy.' I'll tell you where to go and you'll go there. I'll tell you what to say and you'll say it. Don't be afraid of a soul. I'll be right there, looking after you." God's Decree. God reached out, touched my mouth, and said, "Look! I've just put my words in your mouth—hand-delivered! See what I've done? I've given you a job to do among nations and governments—a red-letter day! Your job is to pull up and tear down, take apart and demolish, and then start over, building and planting.*

This was the first scripture I had ever read in the Bible and the Lord led me to this scripture at the age of 22 as I was sitting on the edge of my bed. *First of all, what does this scripture even mean?* was my first thought. Well, I was about to find out up close and personal in the immediate days, months and years to come.

I never told God I wanted to be a prophet, so why was He talking to me about such a thing? I had witnessed many men and women speak a word over me and others and for a minute, I thought it was the most exciting thing, until God started using my lips of clay to speak His oracles. For the life of me, I cannot figure out why people want so bad to be a prophet. Don't they know the cost that comes with the office? Don't they know that in biblical times, prophets were killed because of the messages God placed in their mouths? Don't they know the enemy will do whatever it takes to keep them quiet? I didn't know at first either, but I found out real quick.

During the COVID-19 pandemic, I learned a lot about myself, my relationship with the Lord and my connection to the church. Every day, the Lord and I had spent insurmountable time together as He began unfolding to me His heart and what He was requiring of me during this time as the world was placed at a standstill. One of the things the Lord and I discussed was the subject of being hurt by leaders and confronting the spirit of Jezebel. Many in the Body of Christ are struggling with this well-organized, demonic entity that has plagued millions across the globe. What the Lord revealed to me was so startling, so startling that I began researching this very topic. It wasn't enough for me to just understand my own personal experiences, but I had no choice but to gather the thoughts from women and men of all ages that had endured the trauma of being spiritually raped by leaders that professed to be a man or woman of God but were actually wolves in sheep's clothing. 2 Corinthians 11:13-15, ESV, *For such men are false apostles, deceitful workmen, disguising themselves as apostles of Christ. And no wonder, for even Satan disguises himself as an angel of light. So it is no surprise if his servants, also, disguise themselves as servants of righteousness. Their end will correspond to their deeds.*

I know that this topic is a touchy subject for many. It's a tough topic to discuss for many leaders because many of them are guilty and refuse to admit that instead of feeding the sheep the Lord entrusted to them, they have the blood of the sheep on their hands—those who have been traumatized by their leaders and have been groomed to believe that either they are in some way at fault for the suffering they have endured, they are being dramatic and just want attention or they are retaliating for not getting what they want from their leader, like a position.

Let me make something PERFECTLY clear: This chapter is NOT about a church member being upset because they did not get a specific position in the church. This is not about someone just having a temper tantrum. This chapter is about those of us who have literally had a face-to-face encounter with sexual assault, child molestation, drug abuse, domestic violence, murder, manipulation, deception, false accusations, slander, verbal abuse, mental abuse, emotional abuse, physical abuse, being controlled, excommunicated, bullied, lied on, misused and mistreated by those who took an oath to care for and feed God's sheep.

Please understand, by no means am I trying to nail all leaders to the cross, but for too long, people have suffered in silence and it's time for all the cards to be laid out on the table where everyone can see the hands that have been dealt to countless people.

Resentment and total disgust with the church is the best way I could describe how I felt toward God and the church after all I had been through. It seemed as if no matter what leader I sat under, the enemy found a way to torment me. Even during times when I did not submit to something that I knew was not God, I was labeled as being rebellious and disrespectful. The spirit of Jezebel will become agitated and will begin to spiritually rape or strip you when you choose to obey God instead of man.

Listen, by no means or any stretch of imagination was I perfect. I admit, I was more than a hot mess but no matter what issues a person may come into the church with, no one deserves to be mishandled, misunderstood, used or abused. It was always my understanding that although no leader is perfect, they are to be held to a higher standard and the church is supposed to be a place where the broken, the bruised, the battered and discarded can go and be safe. In my case and in many others' cases, the church has become not a place of safety but a slaughterhouse.

I am not ashamed to say that it took well over 20 years for me to break free and decapitate Jezebel. For me, it took a lot of prayer, seeking the Lord for instructions, allowing God to show me through others that it was time for me to break free and finally discover who I was. Was I scared in the beginning to confront what was trying to destroy me? Absolutely, but the word of the Lord spoke to me so clearly in Philippians 4:13, NKJV: *I can do all things through Christ who strengthens me.*

Here are some red flags that will help you identify if you are under toxic leadership or in alignment with a Jezebel spirit that has been sent to spiritually rape you of your destiny and purpose.

If a leader seems to want to control every aspect of your life, key examples would be:

- Your leader wants to know what's going on in your personal life or marriage and gives you ungodly advice that causes division and/or strife within your relationship
- You are not allowed to visit any other ministry without their permission
- Your leader shared your personal business and they used it against you
- Your leader will cause the church members to stop speaking to you and come against you
- Your leader will try to isolate you
- Your leader will bring in false prophets to spew deception over the congregation

- You feel unproductive and depressed after leaving your leader's presence
- Your leader has released a word curse over your life
- Your leader belittles you and tries to intimidate you
- Your leader tries to control your children
- Your leader tries to convince you that if you leave the church, you will not be able to make it without them
- You feel like you are unable to speak what God is saying; you feel muzzled
- You cannot make any decisions for your life without consulting them first
- Your leader will promote you in order to get what they want from you

Finally, I say to those of you who found yourself in this chapter, no one has a right to control you. God made you an individual for a reason, and He did not make any mistakes when He created you. You have His DNA running through your veins and there is nothing the enemy can do to change that. I pray that you will make a wholesome decision to fight for the call on your life. You have to execute Jezebel, dethrone her and take your voice back. You deserve to be free and you deserve to live to see the promises God has made you. Don't allow any man or woman, no matter what position or office they hold, to stop you from being who and what God has said you are. There are people assigned to you and waiting for you to take that leap of faith that will lead you to your promised land.

God Bless You,
Patasha

Dedication

In memory of my beloved father, Paul Burston, Sr. You were more than my father; you were my greatest supporter, my encourager, the strong force in my life and the one who stood by my side no matter what. Thank you for never giving up on me and loving me until the day you went to sleep in the arms of the Lord. I miss you so much, Dad, and your baby girl is finally free!

Love,

Your Daughter

"Loving yourself is healing
the world."

Jaymie Gerard

Evangelist **Vickie R. Patterson,** is a Certified Spiritual Life Coach, owner of Viktorious International Enterprise and Victorious Moms Doula Services, Founder of Victorious Moms Mentorship, a Mary Kay Beauty Consultant, and Founder of Victorious International Outreach.

Chaplain, Mentor and Motivational Speaker. Vickie has been a Motivational Speaker for several years at the Onondaga County Justice Center, she co-created Anti Violence Trauma Prevention, for the Live and Let Live program. She mentored youth who had a parent that was incarcerated. Vickie has spoken at Syracuse University School of Social Work and at a local high school to empower girls. She held Our Family Response to Violence is Prayer and Peace, in memory of her nephew who was killed due to gun violence.

Vickie enjoys serving the women and children as a birth worker in her community. She provides resources to people that are experiencing homelessness. Her mission is to empower, engage, equip, and uplift those she comes in contact with. She resides in Syracuse, NY with her two daughters and her granddaughter. Vickie is passionate about youth and empowering them to live a peaceful and productive life.

HOW DEEP IS YOUR LOVE?

Vickie Patterson

Introduction

I am excited to share with the readers of this chapter, "How deep is your love?" my journey of faith, forgiveness, perseverance and survivorship. We learn whichever life lessons we are meant to at that time. These life lessons often are teachable moments on the journey of life. As we master our life lessons, they become learned lessons that have been presented to us. We find ourselves repeating many of life's lessons. Hopefully, throughout this chapter you will gain insight and tools to become successful in embracing the lessons and grow into a better person.

Our life lessons can be very heartbreaking and painful. Once you've experienced healing from those painful experiences, a great awakening in the soul and spirit can occur within, as we are evolving into our best self in a loving and healthy way. This has been my personal experience. My faith has been vital to my very existence and overcoming many of life adversities. My parents made sure that I regularly attended the church as a child. This is how my moral foundation was deposited in my spirit and I began my relationship with the Lord. The Biblical principle, *train up a child in the way he should go (teaching him to seek God's wisdom and will for his abilities and talents), and even when he is old, he will not depart from it.* Proverbs 22:6, AMP, in this current era of time that we are experiencing, can give the future generations a solid moral foundation.

Forgiveness is a great gift to yourself and others who have wronged you intentionally, from the spiritual perspective, and as well as the positive physical and health outcomes. I will share my experiences of forgiveness, and the positive results I have gained in this process. The overflowing freedom in my spirit and soul has been worth going through this process of healing. I was freed from the negative emotions such as anger, bitterness, resentment, and emotional pain, which had imprisoned me.

If you are experiencing unforgiveness or other negative emotions, my earnest prayer for you is that you receive hope and courage to release any unforgiveness, bitterness, resentment, and anger. Whatever is keeping you from living your best life internally as well as externally, I encourage you to give yourself permission to let it go. Your choice is the key for you to start experiencing a deeper love for God, yourself and others. Yes, everyone has their own healing process to go through and grow through. If I did not possess resilience, you would not be reading this chapter right now. I am grateful that my faith in God has kept me grounded through the adversities that I've faced in my life. Choosing to forgive others, even when forgiving them did not make logical sense to me, when many were not even remorseful or apologetic for their actions or were harmful to me, was very difficult at times. Through God's strength and love, I was able to forgive people who had wronged me, no matter what the situation. This process did not happen overnight for me. I grew into an understanding of what Romans

8:28 truly means to me: *And we know all things work together for good to them that love God, to them who are called according to his purpose.* According to this biblical truth all things are working for my greater good. Loving God is vital; add the application of this biblical truth to your life.

How Deep is your Love?

I received a message from an individual thanking me for helping with the start of their journey to recovery, 23 years ago. I pondered some of the things that transpired before that recovery start date. Oh, what a journey I had experienced. This title, "How deep is your love," has allowed me to discover and dig deeper into what love truly means to me in my faith, God, self, others, and community. Disclaimer: I am not an expert on love, merely inviting you to see it from my perspective.

The meaning of love can be totally different from one person to the next. The dictionary meaning of love is a feeling of strong or constant affection for a person. The meaning of deep according to Merriam Dictionary is reaching far below the surface; to a thorough extent or profound degree; deeply committed.

This is what love means from the spiritual context. Seven distinct Greek words describe various kinds of love. Have you experienced any of these? Agape love means empathetic, universal love. Eros is erotic, passionate love. Philia is intimate, authentic friendship. Ludus is playful, flirtations love; storge is unconditional, familial love. Philautia is self-love. Pragma is committed, companionate love. Now that you have a defined explanation of love, spiritually and naturally, let's take a deeper look into the love of God.

Every person born into this world has a purpose of existence. *For I know the plans I have for you, declares the lord, plans to prosper*

you, and not harm you, plans to give you a hope and a future.
Jeremiah 29:11, NIV. God is love; the word of God states in 1 John
4:8, AMP, *The one who does not love has not become acquainted
with God (does not and never did know Him) for God is love. (He is
the originator of love, and it is an enduring attribute of His nature.)*
What a blessing it is to understand the depth of God's love for each
of us. *But you, Lord, are a compassionate and gracious God, slow to
anger, abounding in love and faithfulness.* Psalm 86:15, NIV.

The love of God is freely given to us, that is how deep the love
of God is.

Self-love means having a high regard for your own wellbeing.
Self-love allows you to accept your own weaknesses along with
your strengths, and to have compassion for yourself as you strive
to find personal meaning and fulfillment in life. Self-acceptance,
self-determination, self-discipline, self-esteem, self-forgiveness,
self-knowledge, self-respect, self-sufficiency, self-worth—all these
are vital for you to have a healthy wellbeing.

What are you willing to sacrifice in order to have a deeper
love relationship with God and yourself? Loving God intimately
is seeking Him through prayer in His presence. This is referred to
as communing with God. Love yourself properly and in return you
can love another person.

What does it mean to love others spiritually? *You should love
your neighbor as yourself (that is unselfishly seek the best or higher
good for others.* Matthew 22:37-40, AMP. This biblical truth, cou-
pled with self-love, gives a true expression of loving from the heart
and image of God. Loving others consists of parents, siblings, children, partners and friends. All of what you read thus far can be
applied to any of these relationships.

Forgiveness

On May 13, 2007, my life changed forever. I received a call from my older sister that her oldest son had been shot. My beloved nephew was 21 years old. It happened on the eve of Mother's Day. His smile would illuminate everyone he came in contact with, and his infectious sense of humor and laugh were hilarious. Oh, how blessed we were to have him as a part of our family. After surgery for the gunshot wound he sustained, he was taken to the recovery room. While we waited patiently for him to pull through, being in critical condition, he eventually succumbed to his injuries from the senseless act of violence. Upon my nephew's death I experienced stages of loss and grief, including shock, facing my emotions, and anger. My journey to learn how to cope with this great loss was necessary to move forward with my life. This was one of the hardest situations I've experienced. About five months later I suffered another loss, my mother passed. My faith in God gave me the ability to continue to move forward through the tears and a broken heart, despite the back-to-back deaths in my family.

About 10 years after the homicide of my nephew, an individual was apprehended for his murder. Eventually, our family was sitting in a courtroom at the murder trial for his death. Justice is what we hoped to receive, and some closure. About a week later a verdict was rendered… Not guilty. The person was free of all charges that he was accused of. Many of my loved ones were in disbelief at the outcome. What would take place in my life two weeks after the murder trial was a true test of my faith as a believer in God. The individual that I had sat in the same courtroom with walked through the sanctuary doors with his wife and children. I was standing in the pulpit. My prayer within was, *Lord of mercy, I need your divine strength right now, God*. God granted my prayer request instantly. What a mighty God I serve. When it was time for those who desired prayer, the individual who was accused of murdering my nephew had come forward to the altar for prayer and I met him there and asked him if I could pray for him. He responded yes. In my heart I had already forgiven him. Now I was afforded the opportunity to outwardly express that mercy and grace that God extends to me on a daily basis to this individual.

No one should come into the house of God and not experience the authentic love of God. I truly experienced a life-transforming encounter on this particular day. As a woman of faith, it is my earnest desire to reflect the image of God. Do I always get it right? No. Yet, through repentance (change of behavior or of actions), the love of God is being perfected in me as a believer. *Above all, intense and unfailing love for one another, for love covers a multitude of sins (forgives and disregards the offense of others).* 1 Peter 4:8, AMP. The lesson of forgiving is continual. The lesson I learned was to forgive not just with words but with my actions.

May the personal true story I've shared give hope to those who have experienced the loss of a loved one due to gun violence. Coping is very difficult when a tragedy has occurred, and I'm by no means minimizing the pain you may by experiencing. I'm offering a healthy coping strategy from my experience in dealing with loss. I'm not a social worker or therapist. I'm an aunt who loved her nephew dearly. Whatever healthy coping method works for you, get the help you need that's available through community resources, whether it's counseling, a support group, or doing something positive in memory of your loved one. I promised myself that I would keep my nephew's memory alive. Our family's response to gun violence has been Prayer and Peace. May God Almighty mend your broken heart and make it whole again. This is my earnest prayer for the person who resonates with this story.

Perseverance

As a single mother raising two young daughters, after being injured, I found myself experiencing situational poverty. As a result, my children were affected by my inability to work for an extended period of time. I was determined to give my children the quality of life I was capable of, within my means. I made sure they had quality over quantity during this period of time. This skill set; my grandmother shared with me when I was in middle school. The greatest gift I gave them was my physical presence in their early childhood education with Head Start Peace, Inc. Determined to be the best mom I could be, I took every training they offered parents and received many certificates during those years and served on the policy council, which I refer to as the CEO for Parents of Peace, Inc. I attended college and graduated as a legal assistant with honors and made the Dean's list. Yes, with two children, as a single mom, I achieved this. I had great life lessons and learning experiences during those years while recovering from my injuries. My perseverance was my saving grace to maintain my family unit. I was blessed to have great support from both of my daughters' godmothers as well as a few close friends and family members. There's a saying: You never know what a person has been through or is going through unless you've walked in their shoes. I found this to be a true because of based on my situation at the time. Offering a person empathy is awesome when you encounter someone having a life situation. I had great visions for my two daughters' and my financial and physical setbacks were not going to hinder their future. I had mustard seed faith. I applied this biblical principle to our lives: *Now faith is the assurance (title, deed confirmation) of things hoped for (divinely guaranteed) and the evidence of things not seen (the conviction of their reality-faith comprehends as fact what cannot be experienced by the physical senses).* Hebrews 11:1,

AMP. The outcome of my situation allowed for many valuable life lessons and experiences as a single mother. I was blessed that both of my daughters thrived academically, and in sports. They graduated high school, and attended college. My oldest daughter is a licensed cosmetologist and entrepreneur at The Cuse Curlfriend. My youngest daughter is a nurse and entrepreneur, her business is Doula for a Queen It's not what I went through that determined their outcome, it's what I believed would happen for them.

A word of encouragement to a single parent: You can still accomplish your hopes, dreams and aspirations that you have for your life, regardless of what circumstances you find yourself in. With determination and tenacity, you will be victorious over obstacles and adversities. You can and will win in life. Speaking positive affirmations when experiencing doubts will help you keep a positive mindset. I'm so grateful to have overcome so many things that were designed to derail my life.

One of my greatest joys is giving back to my community. Through being a community advocate, a Doula (Birth Worker) serving women and children in my community, I'm always honored to be invited into that sacred space with a mother while she's birthing a child into this world. The moral of this story: My entire family has risen above the setbacks that happened in my life when they were little girls. You or your family can do the same thing too. Keep persevering in your life and always tell yourself giving up isn't an option, no matter what you're faced with in life.

Survivorship

My survivorship consisted of surviving toxic relationships, realizing at the time that they were draining me mentally, emotionally, psychologically and spiritually. These experiences were very subtle. I was not loving myself properly by remaining in these relationships. Those particular relationships added no value to my existence in a healthy way. I had to learn it was ok to release these individuals. The result: I'm now a happier and healthier person. I chose to love me and always do what was best for my life and future. I've survived job loss, not realizing a greater opportunity was on the horizon for me. I tapped into my God-given talents and abilities. This has been the greatest rediscovery in my life. I'm excited to see how my new ventures will unfold and how it's going to bless my family, community and the world.

When we take risks in life, having courage will be necessary. We must not settle for just surviving but thriving as well. We must also constantly be thriving in all areas of our lives. This is a testament of how deeply you love yourself, to keep evolving into who God destined you to be and fulfilling your purpose for existence and positively impacting people, places and things with your presence, on your journey of life, leaving a legacy for future generations that will be grateful that you lived your life out loud. Often, individuals live their lives and never experience the love of God. Or they were not taught how to love themselves. I realized this while talking with many women and men from different age groups.

In this chapter tools and biblical insights were shared; regardless of your age or gender, they can be applied to your life. Every life lesson has brought me to this current place in my life and made me who I am today. It took faith, forgiveness, perseverance and survivorship to be a resilient Black woman shaping the world with my faith. It took a lot of courage to share my story with you. I trust that God will get the glory out of my life. The moment I said yes to writing, I wasn't prepared for what transpired in the days to come. I wanted to quit. I knew this wasn't an option for me, and merely a thought that I wouldn't carry out. This assignment allowed me to confront past hurts in my life, experience love on a deeper level from God, conquer my fear by doing something I've never done before, casting out things that were still trying to attach themselves to me. I'm celebrating completion of this writing. May you receive healing, strength, peace and unspeakable joy in your life.

Upon completion of this chapter, you can now share "How deep your love is" without hesitation, with a fresh new perspective and point of view. Always remember, you are loved by God and He has great things in store for your life. *Trust in and rely confidently on the Lord with all your heart and do not rely on your own insight/ understanding. In all your ways acknowledge and recognize him (God) and he will make your paths straight and smooth (removing obstacles out of your way).* Proverbs 3:5.6, AMP

Dedication

I would like to dedicate this book to the memory of my mother, the late Shirley E. Patterson, my father, Clifford E. Patterson, my Queen Daughters Shakera and SeQuoia, my Tribe, Grand Princess Jaelynn Victoria. Also to the memory of my nephew Silas Keith and my daily inspiration and motivator Stephanie Bee. To my dear friend Latoya Parsons, thank you for your unwavering love and support. Alice Young, cousin, and my bestie Connie Hearns, my Threshing Floor sister and prayer partner. Chief Apostle Betty Gilmore, Call to Pray Ministries, thank you for your love and great spiritual wisdom. Pastor Nadine Days, New Life Christian Church, thank you for your unwavering love, mentorship and being a blessing to my life. Most of all I thank my Heavenly Father for His faithfulness, grace and mercy and unfailing love for me as his Kingdom Daughter. To my future husband, I'm thanking God in advance for an anointed, blessed kingdom marriage. I look forward to meeting you one day very soon. God's timing is perfect.

"Let it hurt. Let it heal. Let it go."

Unknown

Tina Simmons has a Master's degree in Counseling and worked as a therapist for two years with people who struggled with substance abuse, collaboratively creating strategies to address the root causes of their addictions. Seeing the devastating effects addiction had on their children, Tina felt it would be more impactful to reach children before they became addicted. She felt the best way to accomplish this was to become a Substitute Teacher, which she considers the hardest job she has ever loved.

Tina wants to be a part of the village raising a child and is standing up for her community by taking the initiative to help raise this generation's children. She is the author of the soon to be released book, "Out of the Ashes: The Other Side of Pain." She resides in Toledo, OH and loves taking long walks in nature.

LOVE AFTER WAR

Tina Simmons

A simple text I received from an unknown number on April 6, 2021, threw my life into a tailspin. That was the day I learned my ex-husband had been having an affair for the past 16 years. Although at the time of the text, we had been divorced eight years, finding out he had a mistress for the last eight years of our marriage was nonetheless devastating. When I saw my ex-husband's name, I knew it was a text originally sent to him that was being forwarded to me. It read: "(his name), I can't believe you would do this to me after we've been together for 16 years..." I couldn't read past the first sentence. I felt as if I'd been gut punched by Mike Tyson. I couldn't catch my breath and started hyperventilating. Once I screamed a few expletives, I inhaled, held my breath and finished reading. A text that sent me into a free fall had no name attached to it, but somehow, I knew exactly who the woman was. It's funny how at some of the weirdest times, we can recall things our parents may have said to us as children. My mother used to always tell me God doesn't leave us in the dark unless we choose to be in dark, and if we choose to be in the dark, He will let us stay there.

I wasn't quite sure what I wanted to say to her or what she was going to say to me, but I knew I had to have a conversation with this woman. After saying a quick prayer, with shaky fingers I hit redial and a woman I had never met answered. Her voice oddly seemed familiar to me. For the next six hours, she introduced her version of her "husband" to me, and I introduced my version of my husband to her. It was clear he was distinctively two different people. I didn't know her version of him, and she didn't know mine. I wanted to hang up the phone because it was much too painful, but the Lord would not allow it. He needed me to hear all of this because it would help put in perspective why my 18-year marriage failed, because I had spent years blaming myself. I was totally numb. Maybe I was in shock, but I do believe had I responded in anger, my emotions would have caused me to completely miss the move of God that would occur as a result of this initial conversation with my ex-husband's mistress.

After we concluded our phone call, I was nauseous, mentally exhausted and completely numb. I wanted to be bitter and angry, but my heart wouldn't let me. My heart would not allow me to turn cold, no matter how much I wanted that to happen. Everything felt so surreal, as if I was having an out-of-body experience. I couldn't even comprehend what was happening. The only thing I wanted to do was sleep, praying that this was simply a nightmare, and all would be back to normal in my world when I awoke. But when I awakened, I wasn't numb. I was full of rage and the spirit of murder fell upon me. At no point have I ever wanted to do someone harm, but I honestly wanted to kill my ex-husband and had I had access to a firearm, I would have done just that. I understand now how easy it is for Satan to manipulate us when we are being ruled by our emotions. I believe I truly snapped. Thankfully, I recognized I was under spiritual attack and immediately reached out to a few trusted intercessors, who girded me up. For about three hours I went to war with the spirit of murder until I was freed.

Over a 30-day span, I had phone conversations with the mistress which completely changed my heart posture. With a heart filled with compassion, I saw a woman who was broken, a woman who had never truly experienced healthy love from a man. The Lord used me to extend His love to her and help absolve the guilt and shame she felt for having the affair. What these conversations with her revealed was the broken parts in her were reaching out to the broken parts in him, and we all were bonded by the trauma of the infidelity. Without healing, the familiar cycle of dysfunction will continue. Although he and I have never spoken since I learned of the infidelity, it is my prayer that each of them will seek healing, will experience agape love and will develop a true relationship with God. While my ex-husband may have lost me as a friend, he did not gain me as an enemy. My heart holds no malice, anger, envy or hatred toward either of them. I would not have thought any of this would have been possible, but I bear witness when God is involved, even the most impossible things are possible.

After the Lord had me disconnect from the mistress, I asked Him the reason for the connection. He explained to me He needed me to truly see this man for who he really was, but more importantly, He needed to expose negative patterns I had been repeating throughout my life, especially with my ex-husband. I was told as I transitioned into my new season, I had to confront these destructive cycles, else I would keep repeating them. To do this, I had to look at the foundation which formed the basis of our marriage. When a marriage starts off with two people who are unequally yoked, it's highly unlikely the marriage is going to last because there is no solid foundation on which the marriage can be built to help sustain the couple when the storms of life come. Consequently, the only thing that can happen is the couple will grow apart. He and I were unequally yoked, and since we didn't have a strong foundation to start off with, nor good soil, it was easier for Satan to gain a foothold. Once that foothold had been established, it was only a matter of time before our marriage crumbled, which took 18 agonizingly painful years.

It wasn't until I began my healing journey that I understood my ex-husband is a narcissist who is extremely emotionally abusive. But I couldn't see any of this because I was so focused on being a godly wife that I was blind to it all. I truly believed it was my Christian duty to hang in there and endure abuse, to love him harder and allow my soul to be crushed for Christ's sake. Those are lies straight from the pit of hell that I believed. I am sure there are a lot of wives who are in similar situations because it has been pounded into our heads how God hates divorce. Yes, God absolutely does hate divorce, but He never intended for His daughters to be abused. We have to stop letting these false spirits make us think we are called to be victims, because we're not. Praying for your abuser does not mean "pray and stay." It means pray for their soul and entrust their punishment to God. My ex-husband's willful, destructive behavior was not my assignment and was not my good, Christian duty to tolerate. I truly thank God for allowing me to straighten my crown and walk away, knowing that under no circumstances do I owe anyone my life that Jesus hung, bled and died for.

In retrospect, I believe it was my having that "stay no matter what" mentality which gave my ex-husband confidence to believe I would forgive him no matter what, and would never leave him, regardless of how badly he mistreated me. Dysfunction in marriage had been normalized for both of us. I watched my mother endure abuse from my father, and he watched his mother endure abuse from his father. Neither woman left, both staying married for over 50 years, until their spouses died. Because dysfunction and toxicity within the confines of marriage had been normalized, neither of us recognized there was anything wrong with our marriage.

After our divorce, because we had developed a friendship and became better friends than when we were husband and wife, we floated the idea of reconciling. Over the course of our 23 years together, we had been recycling destructive patterns. I now understand how the enemy uses familiarity to get us to reconnect with people he uses to distract us from our Kingdom assignment(s). Had we reconciled, all we would have done was recycle our pain and keep bleeding on each other. This is a manipulative tactic Satan frequently uses which keeps many people bound.

As I was being prepared to enter into my new season, the Lord needed me to be able to forgive and extend grace to someone I thought was completely undeserving. How many times as believers do we extend conditional grace, contingent upon whether WE think the person is worthy? God's grace is never conditional. As His ambassadors on the earth, neither should ours be. Every person sins every single day, yet our merciful God freely extends forgiveness and grace unto us, daily. So how can we not extend the same grace that has been so freely given to us?

My faith has been challenged immensely by what has been one of the most painful experiences of my life, but it has resulted in my gaining strength I never before would have thought possible. Talk about being crushed. No one really wants to endure God's crushing process. But it's through the crushing that we get the valuable oil that can't be obtained any other way. It has been through this crushing that my emotions were stabilized and God tenderized my heart to be sensitive to the brokenness in others. Often, we as women lose ourselves in relationships and marriages, especially when it comes to sex. So often our sole focus is on pleasing a man that we not only neglect our own hearts and desires, but also God's desire for us and how He made us as women. Because so many women confuse lust with love, many become controlled by their emotions and aren't able to govern them, preventing them from experiencing wholesome love, tenderness and care from the man God has for them.

One of the things God kept challenging me with during this time was not to be like Lot's wife. At first, I didn't understand what He meant, but then it became very clear. I was stalling in my healing because I was so focused on why the infidelity occurred. I beat myself up relentlessly because I never saw the betrayal coming. I wondered if it was because I was naive, too busy working, too busy with school, too busy taking care of the family or so heavenly bound that I wasn't paying attention to what was going on right under my nose. I kept looking back, trying to make it make sense to me. Because I understand marriage is a covenant instituted and designed by God from the beginning of time, I really wanted my marriage healed and restored. That's why I was contemplating reconciliation, even though we divorced after years of emotional abuse. And this is why the betrayal hit me so hard, because I understood our covenant in the eyes of God was already broken long before the divorce. Moving on after infidelity is really hard, but I am moving on, step by step, day by day. The reality is it really doesn't matter why the infidelity happened. What matters is I will no longer keep looking back. I am moving forward in my healing.

I am in a period of transition, and as we all know, change is not easy or comfortable. One of the things I am learning through all of this is I have to resist the urge of wanting to stop the process when it gets too uncomfortable or seems to be taking too long. This is where trusting God really matters. Sometimes what appears as chaos in the natural is actually God transitioning us and repositioning us for our next level. The conversations I had with the mistress helped me to recognize I was transitioning, and to accept it more easily. I'm glad I did because it prepared me for what would happen next. When God is taking you to a new dimension, you will have to choose between your old life and the unknown, the familiar versus the unfamiliar. You will have to choose between dimensions because your future starts when your history ends.

A beautiful thing happened after I began to extend grace to the mistress. I found it much easier to extend the same level of grace to my family. My relationship with my mother and three sisters had been fractured since my father's death four years ago, and the fracture had grown almost to the point of being irreparable. I had not spoken to my youngest sister in six months, which meant our children and grandchildren were caught up in the chaos, as well. After years of recycling pain and destructive patterns from our difficult childhood, none of us knew how to interact with each other in a healthy manner. All we knew how to do was bleed out all over each other by continuing in the dysfunctional roles we had as children. We did not understand the toxic relationship patterns in our family, nor did we understand how these dynamics affected our children and grandchildren.

All that changed when I began to extend grace to the mistress. I thought if I could extend grace to her, surely I could extend grace to my family. And that's what I did. I reached out to my youngest sister, who told me God had been dealing with her, too. We agreed to model grace to our family, believing they would follow suit. And they did. My sister and I committed to be the change we wanted to see in our family. Change begins with us, and we have to be willing to take the first step to be the change agent. As with marriage, God honors family and that is why Satan hates both marriages and families. He works relentlessly to undermine the home by doing whatever he can to destroy families. My family very nearly was a casualty, but God has called me to be the bloodline breaker in my family, so I have been standing in the gap for years, warring for my bloodline. I stand in awe witnessing the healing, reconciliation and restoration that is occurring in my family. I only wish my father were alive to see it. I know God is not done with us yet, but this certainly is a good start in a new beginning for my family.

What happened, happened. I harbor no anger or ill will toward anyone because I understand Satan is the REAL ENEMY and he has one goal: to steal, kill and destroy. But I can defeat the devil and live victoriously in Jesus Christ. I can testify that God truly has given me beauty for my ashes, and everything has worked out for my good. God is a Promise Keeper, and He has been faithful in keeping His promises made to me. I lack no good thing. I do feel as if I have been in a major war and am now coming out on the other side with a heart that is bursting with love. I have a supernatural peace that surpasses all understanding. When I was in despair, God came to see about me. He did not leave me to figure it out on my own because I would have made a mess of things. The infidelity caused an insurmountable amount of pain, but it shaped me into a warrior.

I am believing what I've gone through has ushered in a new season of manifested victory in my life. This season will bring forth fruit that has been held back by the enemy, and I believe God is in the process of restoring the years the devil tried to steal from me. It is so important that we stay in the presence of God, because that is the only way for us to remain undisturbed by all that goes on around us. The Lord will protect the hearts of those He holds dear by holding us close to His heart. As He refines our hearts, He will keep us protected. When we get plugged in to the Kingdom of God, we cannot possibly hold on to the victim seat. As citizens of the Kingdom of God, we have access to all of the resources of God's Kingdom. God wants us powerful. He wants us plugged in to Him! God wants to teach us to do His Will, but it is up to us to be synchronized and syncopated to Him.

Sometimes we don't understand why life is the way that it is. We don't understand the reasons why people do the things that they do. At times things don't go the way we planned them, and God seems like He's a million miles away. But what I know for sure is in time God reveals all things. We need to just be still, stand in love and pay attention. When I look back over my life, I stand in awe of God's Amazing Grace, which has always kept me protected. No one has ever loved me the way that God does. In my spirit, mind and body, I surrender myself daily to God. This journey has been so sweet. I have learned to love myself, accept myself, forgive myself, respect myself, believe in myself and be myself. I don't regret yesterday, because yesterday made me who I am today. I never knew God's Amazing Grace has always been my constant friend. I am free of anger. I am free of fear. My mind is at peace. My heart is free to love, free to soar. Amazing Grace saved my life.

It is my prayer that my testimony will inspire, strengthen and equip you to view your life and relationships through fresh eyes. I pray you will gain a new perspective to see yourself as God sees you and that you will begin to reevaluate every relationship. May God reveal areas where healing is needed and may you find the courage to be healed. Peace and grace be unto you.

Dedication

This chapter is dedicated to women in emotionally abusive relationships who think they are alone. You're not!

 **Angela Woods** is a new aspiring author, an entrepreneur ambassador, and single mother of a handsome son, Isaiah, who is autistic. She is a loving, kind, and passionate woman who is looking to motivate and inspire other special needs mothers in need of support, in any way possible, in everyday life. She had an opportunity to speak in two international summits, and has been interviewed on a Facebook Live group, "Life Along the Spectrum."

Angela is in the process of starting a non-profit support group with two colleagues/sisters/girlfriends, which will allow their intellectual, disabled children, to assist in establishing a legacy. Angela's mission is to inspire single mothers via coaching, mentoring, and consulting, letting them know that there is a light at the end of the tunnel. Angela is dependable, authentic, and very compassionate when it comes to caregiving for those who she loves. She is also a huge enthusiast of self-care. She states, *If you don't do it for you, no one else will. Self-care is very important in assisting and managing your mental health journey.*

SHATTERING GENERATIONAL CURSES ONE ANGEL AT A TIME

Angela Woods

Authentic messenger of God Necessary to spread the Gospel gentle as a giant, Easy going, Loyal Achiever equals: Angela Woods

My daily affirmation spells out my birth name, Angela. It wasn't until June 2021 that I took it upon myself to Google the meaning of my name to put on a social media platform as my bio, so I could be introduced to the world as a newly inspired entrepreneur. Forty-nine years of living and I never knew the meaning of my name given to me to use as a method of identification. What about you? Have you ever looked up the meaning of your name so you can have a baseline knowledge of yourself? Wouldn't you like to know if your name matches your personality? If you are curious like everyone who wants to know as opposed to those who don't want to know what their name means, I suggest you do your research. Just say, Hey Google, and ask the meaning of your name. It's Jetsons easy thanks to technology nowadays.

I know what you are probably thinking, why is she asking me to do the above exercise? It won't hurt; it may help you get out of a lonely, sad and dark place that may occur at any time in your life, as happened in my life.

Beauty is in the eye of the beholder, by Margaret Wolf Hungerford, was a mantra I embedded in my brain as an inside personal tattoo.

As long as I can remember a smile was worth gold, more precious than silver, brighter than diamonds, a code of trust. When the trust is broken, you may experience multiple good and bad flare-ups at the same time, and you are left to fend for yourself with no way out or even feeling distraught. Everyone is born with a personal toolbox from God, tools needed to live the way God intended you to live. However, if you don't know how to use them it will cause you to go way off track and getting back on track was never meant to be easy, it just has to be done. The old saying, going two steps forward only to get pushed four steps back, that is not the way to go, plus it makes you feel uncomfortable, not worthy of being alive and downright hopeless.

As I look back over my life, my mental health has been tested, tossed and turned upside down like a rollercoaster. I'm going to take you on a journey that may seem like a fairy tale to some, and others may connect with the words from my heart. You may want to get comfortable, get some tissues, your favorite beverage or a snack—however you choose to read this next chapter. I will wait. Ready? Let's begin…

Lately, I have been sitting and thinking of a time in my life when I was a five-year-old girl, shy, with pigtails in her hair, mud pies in her pocket for sale, while bringing the world around her a ray of sunshine with her smile, her naiveness and her innocence, to name a few, only to be let down by the very people she thought loved her and who she truly trusted. This is not a bashing, tell-all chapter, it is an eye opener for many generations before me and definitely after, who have lost their voice they didn't know existed. The following chapter will give you insight into the first chapters of my past life God intended for me and how I finally grew up to become the woman I am now, a mother to my special angel son Isaiah and a newly inspired author and entrepreneur. I pray that it will inspire, elevate and motivate someone to look at their life and say it's time for me to shine for God, no matter what happens. Sit back and enjoy.

Tested

Being tested back in the day was horrible and I would not have wished it for my enemies. Forgiveness is one of my super-power tools given to me by God to show the world He is real. Dealing with life thirty-three years without the proper guidance and support led me to six years of finding myself, by myself, and led me to writing this chapter. It is time for the generational curses in everyone's life to exit stage left and allow the new person to shine like they are intended to by God.

My first test I can remember was being sexually abused by someone I had to trust on one finger, forgive on another and try to have my brain forget the whole situation, plus not saying a word to anyone, not even my mother. Talk about peer pressure, not by my peers or family member but by my babysitter. An older couple in the neighborhood of Southwest Philadelphia, was highly recommended by neighbors for their home-based childcare babysitting services. After school, I was to go to a place my parents trusted which was around the corner from my house and stay there until I was picked up to go home. One day while everyone was outside the house, I was held back to stay inside for what I thought was to assist with the smaller kids by helping out where I could, a motto

I lived by, only to be taken advantage of. My innocence unplugged and I was not able to process what was going on or how to deal with my emotions. I didn't know how it was supposed to feel, being touched by someone other than my parents when necessary. It made me feel uncomfortable and sad. For two years, I lived in my own bubble, trying to digest what was going on and being a kid at the same time. I did not know how to handle all of my mixed emotions, I was 11, for God's sake; holding it in was another one of God's super-power tools. I thought it was the only way to cope and deal. My coming to terms with this made me sad on the inside and hard-looking on the outside at 49 years of age. I really did not like smiling growing up. My breakthrough was when we moved away, and I was able to enter high school as a scorned and wounded puppy but with an opportunity to turn my life around for the better. In my junior year of school, I was able to join the drill team, a group of females and our director/sponsor, to make a name for myself. My love for music helped me open up and enjoy life to the fullest, especially at church concerts and school musical events. They kept me from drifting down the wrong path and gave me a new chapter in life to fill. Singing of various songs and genres assisted in my understanding about life and responsibilities. In the lyrics of the songs, I remembered each note on a stanza and every emotion felt as I exhaled to my happy place.

Do you remember your happy place? It is a place where you go get away from everyday strife. There were days that I did not want to go on and then my faith in God put me back on track by saying, never give up. When I was a young child growing up, my grandfather, the preacher, instilled in me the basic tools I needed to live my life, to fulfill my responsibilities needed to live a good life. This led me to pursue college. Yes, a woman of color wanted to go to school to learn something new and improve herself. I was given an opportunity to experience a college internship at Walt

Disney World in Orlando, FL in the early 1990s. It became one of the most exciting times of my life. I was able to leave the nest of Philadelphia, PA to make a name for myself. At my first college internship I had to share an apartment with five other cast members and be responsible for myself. That meant learning how to pay rent, get to work on time, grocery shopping, and budgeting, plus sharing community space. After doing two internships back-to-back I realized I wanted to live on my own; the only thing that stopped me was my fear. I had an opportunity to stay in Florida with family, but I got homesick and missed my mother.

Tossed

This brings me to being tossed, two months after my 24th birthday, in March of '96. I learned I was two months pregnant after a night out of drinking and partying with co-workers. I couldn't keep any substance down; I felt queasy most of the time. Feeling that bad and knowing I had to keep working, I did not like calling out from work regularly. I went to my family doctor to get his opinion and oh boy, did I get it. Without doing a simple test of any kind, I was given a diagnosis of pregnancy, something so shocking that I went numb! The doctor asked me a bunch questions that I answered so diligently that pregnancy never crossed my mind. I ended up walking 14 blocks to my neighborhood CVS Pharmacy so I could purchase an over-the-counter pregnancy test. What makes this a tossed situation is I had to grow up ASAP and make some life-changing decisions that would affect my future forever. Abortion and adoption were not options, so I had to put my big girl panties on and trust in God my savior and deal with the notion of motherhood. If you are a parent, then you can relate to my emotional rollercoaster and being blind-sided.

This next part of our rollercoaster ride is where I learned how patience is another tool in my toolbox of life. Another time I was tossed was when I realized I needed help with my mental health. I sat alone in my two-bedroom apartment in the dark, crying for two hours. What could possibly bring me to that low point, you might ask? I have come to believe God has a sense of humor. I never wanted children. The word 'never' was ingrained in my vocabulary. I would say it out loud, under my breath or even in my silent prayers. I used the word "never" so much that it came true with the birth of my son, Isaiah, which shows you my resilience, my perseverance and my high level of patience. The second part of my tossed life was the day my son was diagnosed with Autism, a neurological brain disorder, attention deficit hyperactivity disorder (ADHD) and Persuasive Development Delay (PDD). I went from a healthy, vibrant, bouncing baby boy to a non-responsive, incoherent, unruly three-year-old. How did this happen to my child? What did I do for my child to act like this? These questions came to my mind, not in a rage or angry attitude, but in a solitude and subtle way. Some people and medical personnel would say that's typical for a child of that age, but it hits differently when you are pulled to the side before picking up your child from daycare by one of your child's teachers to hear her say, "Ms. Woods we need to discuss some things about your son." As a first-time mother, I was taking advice from anyone I trusted and whoever was giving it out; like the old saying, "babies do not come with instructions." So every piece of advice to help better myself and my child would be appreciated, recognized and graciously rewarded.

Turned

At the beginning of my chapter, I noted I was taking you on a roll-ercoaster ride. As you can see, the ride can place you in neutral or on cruise control while handling God's unforeseen life plan, that may have you questioning yourself and your creator. You may not like the answer or consequences of the karma that may come your way to distract you and cause you to get off balance. I was raised to never question God. My faith in the God I serve has kept my head above water no matter what I was dealing with. It brought me to be around like-minded people to help me prepare for this very moment in this time of my life. This anthology project has opened my eyes wide, to see a bigger and better picture of life in hopes those who will read it would be changed for the better. Going back to God, the creator of all mankind, and asking Him for the necessary understanding of His word, to assist and build the life needed to shine, will be the greatest accomplishment you could ever do for yourself.

With that being said and to show you, my reader, a miracle of God, this chapter is the first of many chapters to come of all the sacrifices I have made, people I have come in contact with and how I made peace with my trauma-induced past so I could live my life abundantly, freely and peacefully.

Imagine living all the above traumatic experiences for 25 years straight, no break, by yourself and all alone—this sounds like the *Groundhog Day* movie with Bill Murray. He lived the same day over and over again until he made a life-changing turn for the better, so he could do better. Presently today, writing this chapter is like giving birth to a new me and the beginning of a legacy for my son. Shattering Generational Curses One Angel at A Time is the start of a new beginning in life for anyone who has dealt with lies, deceit and secrets in their family. There may be backlash and resentment to the family member who is stuck on the shelf, watching and waiting for you to fail rather than helping uplift you to your highest potential. Strength in numbers is more powerful than by yourself, alone; that is where networking, stepping outside of your comfort zone and being okay with it and having a passionate outlook on life comes in.

As I close my chapter, I pray it wasn't too disturbing for the weak at heart, knowing the rollercoaster ride I was placed on by God stays on cruise control, with the ability to stop and smell the roses. This anthology project was the best thing for me to be involved with and gave me a chance to find myself and be okay with the outcome.

Do you know who you are? What generational curse is haunting your family and your life? Can you be okay with life if you don't know what haunts you, but want to move on in life to show yourself to God? Being tested, tossed and turned has given me a second chance in life and I plan on being what God intended me to be, His personal messenger. Step outside your comfort zone to get to the next level of life; you can thank me later. Invest in yourself, don't wait on anyone, be the leader so someone else can do the same. Read the poem "Deepest Fear" by Marianne Williamson; consult the people who know you and who have been in your life the longest. Wisdom comes with time. Life is not a sprint, it's a marathon. It has been my pleasure and honor to take you on a partial journey of my life and I am ready for whatever God has planned. Never give up, never give in. You are worth it. I AM too. Amen.

Dedication

This chapter is dedicated to my God, my savior, and my village who helped raise me and gave me the knowledge and expertise on raising my son, my responsibility. Thank you, Angela.

"If you are always trying
to be normal, you will
never know how amazing
you can be."

Maya Angelou

Tawisha Nikki Buckingham is a mother of two and a grandmother of two. She was born and raised in Upstate NY but later relocated to the state of Georgia with her family through a job promotion and transfer with her employer in 2006. Tawisha is a Bachelor of Arts graduate in Political Science from the State University of New York at Buffalo and is due to complete her Master's in Healthcare Administration in April 2022 at the University of Arizona.

Tawisha is a proud woman of God, a member of Wesley Chapel United Methodist Church in McDonough, Georgia where she is also a member of the Usher and United Methodist Women auxiliaries. Tawisha is a contract negotiator at a Fortune 500 healthcare organization where she's been an employee for 14 years. Tawisha enjoys the beach, reading, outlet mall shopping, spending time with family and anything pertaining to self-care and peace.

HOLDING GOD'S HAND THROUGH THE STORM: WALKING INTO HIS WILL WITH FAITH

Tawisha Buckingham

As a junior in college, I had my goals and plans in place for this thing called LIFE. I wanted to go to college and become an attorney, get married by age 27 and have my first child at 30.

I was adamant about this plan and spoke on it quite frequently to myself and to my peers. I wanted what people would call the 'perfect' life. After completing high school, I enrolled at SUNY Buffalo in Buffalo, NY and majored in Political Science, with an English minor, which was what was considered the best prerequisite for law school at that time.

After completing almost three years of college, I became pregnant. For someone who always "had her stuff together" and always "remained studious and focused," I felt completely lost and scared. I felt confused and hopeless with the thoughts that my life and future were over. I was too nervous to tell my family, particularly my mother, what had occurred and even considered the possibility of not moving forward with the pregnancy. For months, a feeling of hopelessness came over me as I carried on with my daily routine despite the reality of a little life growing inside my womb. One day some friends and I went to a nearby mall and as we walked into the entrance of the mall there was a glass mirror the length of the hallway preceding the mall's double glass doors. As I walked past the mirrors, I glanced at myself and saw a noticeable baby pooch. I told myself that if I could see the baby pooch, then they could see the baby pooch. I did not share the news with anyone at the time. Only the father of my child and I knew. At that very moment was when it hit me that I was carrying another human being in my belly and reality set in my mind that I was going to be a mother (although Planned Parenthood confirmed for us several weeks prior). This is the moment I stopped running from my reality. My child's father was excited about the new bundle of joy, but I still had not discussed with my family and I was still lost in my new reality. After leaving the mall and riding home in the back seat of my friend's car, I was hit with the realization that it was time to pull myself up by the "bootstraps" and handle my most important business, motherhood. God had placed not only a human seed in me, but He also placed a spiritual seed in me.

I made the choice to move forward in life with God's most precious gift, my child. I decided to remain in college, in the classroom setting, while pregnant with my child. In the process, I arranged with each of my professors to take a six-week "maternity leave" in my second semester in college so that I could remain abreast of my coursework yet also take the time to recover from delivery and return to classes to complete the semester in April. Furthermore, I chose to continue with college to earn my Bachelor's degree in lieu of withdrawing from college to marry the father of my child, which was a difficult decision to make, but I needed an education more than ever at that point. With the solid support system of my aunt, who was a stay-at-home mother, I was forced to make another difficult decision after giving birth: to leave my newborn baby boy, Voiese Jr. (VJ), at six weeks with her and my uncle while I returned to school three hours away to finish the Spring semester. God is awesome. As I traveled home each weekend, He assured that the weather permitted so that I could love on my new baby boy (we all know that it can snow into the Spring months in Upstate New York). God also cleared the path so that I was safe traveling on the highway each week. God will always make a way when we are obedient to His will.

Isaiah 1:19, ESV - *If you are willing and obedient, you shall eat the good of the land.*

The summer went by quickly as I completed my internship with UTC Carrier Corporation and nervously prepared for my senior year in college. I was under the circumstances where I had no choice but to bring my six-month-old child with me to school.

Of course, we were not allowed to live in the dorms with our children. Fortunately, at the last minute, I was able to find an off-campus apartment and my uncle loaded his truck up and dropped us off in Buffalo. The first couple of weeks were tough, as I only had college friends at school, who were also enrolled in classes and were unable to participate in 'babysitting' duty while in classes during the day. I had a new baby that did not sleep at night and my first class was at 9 am. I recall crying when having to get up for class with only three hours of sleep. In addition to sleepless nights, I was pulled to the side by one of my professors, advising me that I was unable to bring my baby boy to class with me again. All in all, I was determined to maintain my class attendance and to remain steadfast regarding my course assignments. After a couple of days, I felt completely overwhelmed and defeated, not knowing how I was going to finish college with a new child literally on my hip each day. I knew that if I were to leave school, I would more than likely not return to finish. With that, dropping out was not an option and dropping out never crossed my mind despite the insurmountable discouragement and odds against me accomplishing my goal of completing my degree. God planted a root in me of stubbornness, refusing to change my attitude and position about obtaining my education and the drive to complete the task, no matter what obstacles came my way.

For he will command His angels concerning you, to guard you in all your ways. Psalm 91:11, NIV. One day I decided to drive in the surrounding area of my campus and as I was driving, I saw a sign for a daycare center. All I could think of was how would I be able to pay for daycare as a full-time college student. I decided to walk in and talk with the daycare director and in the process, I learned that the day care center was Black-owned. Although very much discouraged about the opportunity to enroll my son due the inability to pay the weekly tuition, I asked about the details of the school and the cost. The daycare owner advised that the tuition was $150 a week. I proceeded to explain to the owner that I was a full-time college student at the University down the street and that I desperately needed daycare services for my son while I was in class during the day. The daycare owner made me an offer that became a turning point in my life. She stated to me that she wanted to help me and that she would charge me only $50 a week for my son to attend the daycare during the hours that I was in classes. I knew at that very moment that God had His hands on me and on my child and placed the right person on my path. I knew that the foundation was laid so that I could complete my required coursework so that I could obtain my degree and ultimately have doors opened for me. So I decided to budget my daycare tuition through my student loan request in my final year in college, which allowed me to focus solely on being a mother and a student. I obtained my degree the following spring, with my one-year-old and family attending my college graduation.

I later went on to have a beautiful daughter, which further rooted a drive in me to excel in a career that would provide my children with a life of comfort and peace in knowing that God would always supply our needs. He encourages us to be diligent workers in whatever career path we choose to take. Being the best example of that to my children as a single mom was my priority. I wanted them to have nothing but the best in life, with God's anointing on it.

I started a path in customer service for four years after college. I enjoyed it and met friends that became family to me and my children. After four years in customer service, I was laid off from a customer service organization, and this forced me to seek new career opportunities. I decided to apply at a temporary agency, where the recruiter aligned me with a major healthcare organization that I had not heard of at that time. The recruiter stated to me that because I had a Bachelor's degree, I would be offered a temporary position with the organization. Once again, God connected the dots for me and proved to me that this degree would be the driving force in my career and that the hard work would pay off. I worked as a temporary employee at this organization for two years before being hired permanently, with benefits. A full-time position in network management was offered; there were over 10 people applying for it, and I was called in by the director advising that I was chosen for the role. He wanted me to know specifically why I was offered the position. He advised that I was the only applicant that had a college degree. Although I have witnessed many people do abundantly well in their careers and entrepreneurships without degrees, it was in God's plan for me to obtain mine and to build a certain character within me through the route He had planned for me in life. After four years working at the healthcare organization in Upstate NY, I accepted a job transfer and promotion for a position in Georgia with the same organization. After one year with the company in Georgia, I was laid off in October.

Worried and very concerned about my family's financial future and after only one year of living in Georgia, I began to diligently pound the pavement in applying for other positions. Moving back home was not an option that I wanted to accept as I relocated to excel in my career and my potential career opportunities were in Georgia. So I began applying for positions with other companies within the same industry, and it paid off. I received a call for an interview from the competitor company and was hired five weeks later in December. God does the orchestration; He will guide our steps and will place us at the right place at the right time. He will provide you with the tools you will need to overcome any battle. I had begun working the first week in December and was not due to receive my first payroll check until the end of December. However, because I began working on an off-payroll week, I received a paycheck the second week in December, enabling me to purchase Christmas gifts for my children. I do not believe in coincidences, as this was what I call a synchronous deed provided to us by God because He is an on-time God. In addition, God has blessed me with the opportunity to establish a solid career at this organization and 14 years later I am still an employee and continuing to leverage God's encouragement and guidance in my position. Moreover, God blessed me with the opportunity to work from home in most of my career, as the company that I work for saw how work-life balance was and is key in managing not only one's professional life but also one's personal life. This aspect of my career allowed for me to be available to my career and most importantly to my family, which I am grateful for. God's hands were and are still in the path of my career and in how I balance work and life, making it more productive and rewarding.

Proverbs 22:6, KJV –*Train up a child in a way he should go, and when he is old, he will not depart from it.* My one and only son, Voiese Jr. (VJ), was the light of our family's world and was a very handsome and very smart young man who marched to the beat of his own drum. He had a smile that lit up any room when he entered it. He was a young man who was far beyond his years and so universally connected at such a young age, I chose to identify him as an angel on earth. VJ exuded wisdom that continues to guide me today. He was an observer and a deep thinker. VJ was a total and complete "mama's boy" and was very proud of it. He made me a very proud mother and was always respectful to those with whom he crossed paths. He carried a light wherever he went and always conducted himself as a leader with confidence. VJ loved hip-hop music and hip-hop culture, which influenced his interest in establishing his own business as a teen. He managed his own clothing line, Clubhouse Clothing, while he was a student in high school and was selected out of many to be a mentee under the 100 Black Men of South Metro Atlanta, Inc. organization. He also attended Valdosta State University with a major in Communications. VJ's charisma and charm contributed to his ability to be an awesome leader amongst his peers. VJ was a loyal friend to many, and it was important for him to support his family and friends if ever needed.

James 3: 14-15, ESV - *But if you have bitter jealousy and selfish ambition in your hearts do not boast and be false to the truth. This is not the wisdom that comes down from above, but is earthly, unspiritual, demonic.* In January 2020, I lost my son VJ to a senseless act of gun violence at the hands of someone that he grew up with as a friend and had known for over 11 years. This was an act of the ultimate betrayal, with roots of jealousy and envy.

Isaiah 41:10, NKJV-*Fear not, for I am with you; be not dismayed, for I am your God; I will strengthen you, Yes, I will help you, I will uphold you with my righteous right hand.* I learned that God will be there for you at your highest in life and He will also be a rock for you when you are at your lowest in life. My biggest fear as a mother of a son was now a reality, my worst nightmare. The pain of losing a child is the most indescribable form of pain. Learning about my son's passing was a complete out-of-body experience that came with total shock and disbelief. My emotions were across the spectrum, with rage and disgust being as high as the overwhelming sadness and complete brokenness. Before losing my son, I thought that I was the closest to God that I could ever get but being forced to continue to live life without my child drew me even closer to Him. My family and I needed God more than ever now. I needed God to hold me, to help me to eat and to sleep and to guide me through, as I knew that we are not to question Him. I needed God to give me the strength to continue to be there for my daughter and grandson and to continue to manage a household. There is nothing too difficult for God. He is the Jehovah El Roi, the God who sees me, and it was the comfort and peace that He bestowed on me **immediately** that kept me sane. He knew exactly what I needed to keep going and to keep pressing in my Faith in Him. Philippians 4:19, KJV, *And my God shall supply all your needs according to His riches in glory in Christ Jesus.*

James 4:8, ESV - *Draw near to God and He will draw near to you.* I have become more connected to the universe, and I have become more alert and aware of my surroundings, which opened me up to receive spiritual communications from VJ in the higher realm, giving me the peace and comfort that goes beyond understanding. I continue to take one day at a time, knowing that God is holding my hand every step of the way. We continue to stay connected to the leaders of our church and to loved ones nearby and far. We continue to lean on God and His word, trusting in His will and His way.

Late last year, my daughter discovered that she was expecting my first granddaughter and was informed some weeks later by her OBGYN team that the baby had a heart condition called tricuspid atresia and will have to go through a series of open-heart surgeries, with the first being at three months old. This news was devastating for us.

Proverbs 3:5, NIV - *Trust in the Lord with all your heart, and lean not on your own understanding.*

Baby Jolani Voiese (her uncle's namesake; "Voiese" means little warrior) decided to enter the world on her own terms on July 24, 2021, arriving two days earlier than her induction date, which was four weeks sooner than her actual due date. She weighed 4 pounds and 6 ounces and was as beautiful as ever. With her heart condition, doctors were concerned with Jolani's ability to maintain enough oxygen throughout her organs, even with support. With this issue, it was decided by the heart doctors and surgeons that Jolani would need to undergo emergency heart surgery to implant a heart shunt at just barely three weeks and under five pounds. The prayer warriors were actively at work and as we awaited its completion, God blessed us with a successful surgery. Although she experienced difficulties afterwards, major loss of blood and cardiac arrest, God placed her in His hands and carried her through. Jolani recovered in the hospital for several weeks and was finally able to come home after being in the hospital for 59 days. There is power in prayer and God gave Jolani the power of David winning the battle against Goliath. We will continue to hold God's hand and trust in His power to heal Jolani as she continues to grow and gain a healthier heart.

The Lord's hand has carried and kept me and my family through it all. Amen!

Dedication

First and foremost, I dedicate this chapter to the Most High, Awesome God. One of the highest callings that God may charge one with is that of a mother. With that, I would like to also dedicate this chapter to my children and grandchildren: Voiese J. Pinn, Jr., Viari J. Pinn, Josiah T. Morris and Jolani V. Johnson. In addition, I would like to dedicate this chapter to the memory and legacy of my son, Voiese J. Pinn, Jr, my first heartbeat, my first inspiration in life, my guardian angel and spiritual guide.

"To accept ourselves as we are means to value our imperfections as much as our perfections."

Sandra Bierig

Sarah Ausby is a mother, a grandmother, and an entrepreneur of multiple businesses. Her chapter reflects her journey from childhood to adulthood. She experienced abandonment, emptiness, depression, low self-esteem, and struggles with her identity before finally achieving abundant love and joy. She was able to navigate through the rough terrains of her life with the support of a few people that God placed in her life. In the end Sarah discovers love of herself and confidence in being just who she was created to be. She exhibits strength and courage despite her fears. Sarah shares intimate details of the challenges she endured and her triumphs. In sharing her story, she hopes to encourage others to never give up, and to know that we all make mistakes but with faith in God all things are possible to those who believe.

MY JOURNEY FROM DEATH TO LIFE

Sarah Ausby

My journey to becoming a daddy's girl began long ago. My mother, Mary Richards, and father, William Tenner, never married but remained friends. My father moved to Chicago, Illinois not long after I was born and lived in the mid-west part of the United States for as long as I can remember. My mother lived in Roosevelt, New York and that is where I was born on a very cold day in December 1969. I was raised in Roosevelt until I was eight years old and then we moved to Freeport, New York, just one town over from Roosevelt. The first memory of my father visiting me in New York was when I was just six years old. At that time, I recall meeting my younger brother, who at the time was turning five years old. I remember that visit as if it were just yesterday, with a feeling of joy and love. As the years went on, I didn't see my father and I didn't know why. I am not certain if I ever asked my mother why he hadn't come back or where he was during that time, but I suppose I did, as most children tend to.

When I was about eight years old, I remember my mother began to attend a local church. The pastor was a cousin of my adoptive aunt. My mother joined the choir and my older sister and I would often go to rehearsal with her. I remember practicing the songs along with the choir on the sidelines as if I were in the choir. One of my older adoptive cousins was also a member of the church choir and I would often attend the rehearsals with her when my mother eventually stopped going. Though my mother didn't attend much anymore, my older sister and I were still sent along with other family members. By the time I was nine years old I was baptized at Mt. Sinai Baptist church in Roosevelt, New York. I don't recall how it was explained to me back then, but it was shortly after that I began to truly be attacked in my life by the enemy. At nine years old I was fondled by my adoptive aunt's husband. He had been fondling me for what seemed like months. When it was discovered, I never saw him again and we never spoke of it again. I began therapy sessions for a very short time as a teenager and in those sessions, we never spoke of what happened. I am unaware if the therapist knew of what took place, but the subject never came up. After that I was damaged emotionally as well as mentally and had no form of release. I felt like I was lost, all alone and that no one cared about me. It was at this time in my life that I began to exhibit mischievous behaviors. By the time I was 10 years old I started praying for God to put me in a new family. I didn't want the one I was given; it didn't appear that I was truly important to anyone in this family.

You see, the devil had begun to convince me that it might even be better if I just wasn't here anymore. I began to hear whispers of things like "just step off the curb in front of a bus and it will be over." But my God had very different plans for me. I do know my mother wanted to do her best in raising my siblings and me, but she had great financial challenges. I believe out of desperation but also faith, my mother began to send my sister and me to church regularly. I enjoyed it but I was mostly fascinated and curious about the pastor's family. I thought that this is what my family should be like;

in reality I had no idea what the pastor's family was like. All I knew was what I saw when I played at their house with the youngest daughter in the family, and as a lost and desperate child that was enough for me. I was a child in distress and no one but God knew how bad it was.

As time went on and I grew, I made a friend, and I was what seemed to be happy. I had never quite fit in and I always felt awkward. So when I met this one girl it felt nice to have a friend, but still I didn't feel totally accepted for who I was. In sixth grade I experienced being bullied by a new girl to our school. My new friend wasn't around during this time. I told teachers, my mother, my older sister and no one could make it stop. Things were different in that time, and I was told by my siblings to just beat her up and she would leave me alone. For some reason, unknown at the time, I just couldn't bring myself to hurt her. No matter how much this girl tortured me, I just could not bring myself to hurt her. I knew she did not know how much rage I had inside me and I was afraid of what I would do to her. One day shortly after that she was gone; that girl left our school. I had been praying for God to help me and I believed that this was His answer. For once I felt like someone heard me and cared.

Even though I had one real friend really to speak of, there was always that voice telling me, "No one really cares about you and you don't matter." The church I was attending at the time did not have anyone I could go to and share my feelings of despair. I wanted help; it just seemed as if I was invisible at the time. Nevertheless, I carried on, wearing the mask of happiness when the situation suited. I began to not attend classes and sneak my sister's clothes to wear and things of that nature. One might say these things are normal adolescent behavior, but I assure you it was anything but. The behaviors became so extreme my mother had given my adoptive aunt guardianship of me. She was in nursing school and raising four children alone and one was quickly becoming an at-risk youth despite her best efforts.

By the time I was 14 years old I had been running away from home and hiding from my family for two years on and off. It was at this time in my life that I had done some of the most dangerous things. I was in places I had no business, with people I had no business, and too young to truly understand it all. My eldest and dearest aunt, Edna Threadgill, continually prayed for me. She would put my name on the prayer list on the radio, and she would always say to me, "God is going to stop those running feet." When I lived at her house, she would sit up waiting for me to come home (many times I did not), so my mother could sleep for her next day's work. There were several people in my family who tried talking to me to see if they could get me to just behave and follow the rules. But their talks, which at the time felt more like speeches, fell on deaf ears—in one ear and out the other, as it has been said. When I was at home, I was required to attend church regularly and I did so, reluctantly.

One night there was a revival at the church, or a special service. I was required to go, and I did again, reluctantly. There was a point where the pastor instructed everyone to stand up and begin to praise God. As a young person, confused, afraid and feeling alone in the world, I figured what could it hurt? So I began to clap my hands and say, "Thank you, Jesus" repeatedly. This went on for some time and the next thing I remember was two of the church mothers standing around me saying, "Bring it into submission, baby." I know some may have their own thoughts on this but for me it was in that very moment that I knew the Lord was real. I was told that I was speaking in tongues, but all I knew is I felt different. And yet my behaviors continued, only now I would do negative things and feel so sorry or wish I hadn't done it. There would be more dangerous situations, but God always provided a way of escape and even when I failed to realize it, He protected me from what could have been. I know that now as an adult.

Around 1984, while attending Roosevelt Jr. Sr. High School, I was in my Earth Science class and there was an incident with my teacher. This class was particularly wild. The teacher was really nice, but the students did not respect her authority. On this fateful day a student began throwing books and one hit me in the head. I quickly turned around with book in hand to throw, not knowing the teacher was bending down, picking something up. I threw the book and it hit her in the head when she stood up. "Oh no!" I screamed. I was sorry, and I didn't know just what I had done. As it turned out, the teacher had a concussion from that incident. I was made an example of that day and I was expelled from school and placed in a group home. The school wanted me punished to the fullest extent of the law. I had been charged with assault and my life was changed forever, again. I was quickly whisked away to the local group home and since I had a history of running away, my shoes were taken upon admission. Again, I would not just accept the rules and what was. I found a way to run away from that place, as well, and hid for several weeks.

Once I was located, I was brought to a detention center for juveniles, where I remained until more permanent housing placement was located for me. This place was a jail for youth; there were cells and bars, with visitation only on approval. I had gotten myself into a situation that was beyond my parents' control, and I wasn't praying much at all. I thought maybe I had done too much, and God was tired of me. I had not been taught that we can fall down and get back up, that He is only a repentance away. Or maybe I wasn't paying close enough attention. All I had to do was ask for Him for forgiveness. I finally heard a small voice inside me saying that I was not alone and I would make it through this. I felt like I could pray and ask God to please help me out of this situation and make me better. That was my prayer. I totally believed that only He could help me. Shortly after that prayer I was taken to a small town in Upstate New York called Esopus. The next closest town was New Paltz. This was a co-ed group home for at risk youth run by nuns.

Even at this stage I still carried on with negative behaviors at various times, though the behaviors weren't as often. It would seem that I was just determined to be rebellious to anyone who appeared to be in a position of authority and didn't pay attention to me. No matter what I did, I could not shake the feeling that I needed to do better and that I was meant to do more with my life. I just didn't understand how or know what I was supposed to do. I had always wanted to help people, but how could I help someone when I need so much help myself? I didn't see how I could help anyone because I was so broken and had low self-esteem. After all, what could I really offer anyone? I had become promiscuous due to the previous unresolved issues regarding the inappropriate touching situation. I had given away my power by allowing myself to be exposed to things I knew were dangerous and wrong. I allowed people to use and abuse me in ways I never thought I would, all because I did not know who I was or to whom I belonged.

As a young girl without the guidance of her father and feeling like she was all alone and no one cared about her, I truly believed that I didn't have a right to say no and that sex was all I really had to offer. So anytime I found myself in a situation where a man was aggressive toward me sexually, I more often than not would just cave into what they wanted at the time. I was so ashamed and embarrassed of my past abuse I did not share with anyone what I was going through. I just suffered through, not realizing I was allowing myself to be destroyed piece by piece. I continued to wear the mask, pretending to be happy, and then it finally happened. I met a man, a man I thought was the man for me. He was very kind to me and thought I was beautiful. We spent time together and after only a short relationship we separated. I would later find out I was six weeks pregnant, and I did not want to share the pregnancy with him for fear of rejection. Also, I didn't want him to think I was looking for him to do anything, though he should, of course. So I carried on and planned on giving birth alone and raising my child alone.

Much to my surprise, my son's father was the opposite of everything I was thinking. He was very supportive and wanted to provide for us both. I remember thinking to myself this was great, as now I didn't have to do it all alone. So on June 28, 1989 I went into labor between 7:00 a.m and 9:00 a.m. at 18 Andrews Avenue, Roosevelt, New York. That was my beloved Aunt Edna's home and I had been living there. I was rushed to the hospital by ambulance and my mother and my aunt met me there. It would take many hours but finally, at 11:48 p.m. I gave birth to my first bundle of joy, 8lbs 14ozs. He would be named Billal, after his uncle on his father's side. I didn't seem to have a care in the world, but this feeling would be short-lived. When Billal was only three months old, his father was arrested and would not be released for five years. I had to do what I feared early on in my pregnancy and raise my child alone. Thankfully I had the support of my family and a few good friends.

After a while I met a "friend" and he also was a short-lived relationship, though the dynamics were very different. This was not a man who cared for me so much but rather needed me to survive at the time, and I needed to be needed. It was a toxic and abusive relationship that thankfully lasted less than two years. The only joy I carried from that relationship is my amazing and handsome son, Rameek. It was extremely rough with two children, and I was only 21 years old, but again I had the support of my family. I had a praying mother and several other praying family members; it was those prayers that carried me through. My eldest sister had been living in Syracuse, New York for several years at this point, and it was thought to be a good change for me. So at my mother's advice I moved; I gathered my children and myself and moved to Syracuse, New York on May 2, 1991. After about one year of living in Syracuse I began to make occasional trips back to Roosevelt.

It was during one of these trips back to Roosevelt that I met my youngest son's father in 1992. We shared a mutual friend and she said he was a great guy. This friend introduced us to one another and after a few visits and us hanging out together, we formed a relationship. In the following months he would move to Syracuse with me. He was great with the children, and they really seemed to like him as well. Before long I was pregnant again. I had strayed so far from my faith by this point I wasn't praying at all. After I gave birth to my third handsome and super intelligent son, Tyrell, our relationship took a turn for the worse and never recovered. We stayed together for almost four years before the relationship eventually dissolved. I was right where God needed me to be at that time.

I began to work at a retail store during the Christmas season in 1994, along with one of my younger sisters. She had moved to Syracuse about one year after I did. One day she was talking about a guy she was dating and how he had a cousin that looked like a famous person I thought was so handsome. After our shift one night she invited me to her house because the cousin, Donald Ausby, was to be there. I went to her house to meet him; we had an instant connection. That man later became my wonderful, now late husband. On one of our first dates, he invited me to church, and God spoke to my spirit. We later married on my birthday in December of 1997 and we had a beautiful, blissful marriage. It was very rough for me after he passed away; he was my best friend. I was having a nervous breakdown and not one person was aware of what I was going through. One of my older cousins was a minister and he would call to check on me. It was during one of those phone calls that I made him aware of what I was experiencing. He prayed with me and I can tell you that every day after that when the children would leave for school, I would fall on my face, sprawled out on the floor, crying out to God.

I write this chapter today as a delivered, redeemed, faith-filled, blessed and highly favored woman of God. It is only by His grace and mercy that I am here today. My Father saved me; I'm a Daddy's girl.

Dedication

I dedicate this chapter to my loving mother, Mary Richards, my late father, William Tenner, my children, Billal Fofanah, Rameek Silas and Tyrell McCreary and my late husband and best friend, Donald Ausby. A special thank you to my cousin, Vivian Battle-Cannon, for being just who you are I love you so much, Rita A. Lawrence for always being there for me and one of my oldest and closest friends, Taska Brewster, for always loving and supporting me.

Angel S. Stanley is a registered nurse with 24 years of experience; who specializes in complex trauma and the stress response. She is a nurse educator and nursing theorist of the Holistic Care Theory. She serves her community as advocate for mental health, Autism, HIV/AIDS education and community wellness. Angel is board certified nurse practitioner in psychiatry; Certified Complex Trauma Specialist; Certified Mental Health Integrative Medicine Provider; Complementary and Alternative Energy Healer; and Addiction Specialist. Areas of research: Complex and Intergenerational Trauma; Trauma and Behavior Development over the Life Span; Neuro-Psychiatry and Epigenetics; Psycho-Social Impact of HIV/AIDS in African American Women; HPA axis and the stress response on psychological and physiological wellness. Angel's current mission is child and adolescent mental health screening, early intervention, access to treatment, and awareness of mental health disparities in the African American Community. Angel is a co-creator of CNY Community Healers, Astrologist and Tarot Reader.

LIVING IN REVERSE: THE HERO'S JOURNEY

Angel S. Stanley

W hat's in a name? A predetermined course of events I identify as my hero journey, like a fool born into the world, naïve and with infinite potential, an empty slate from which to create. If you ask my mom who chose my name, she would say her but my father always said him. Either way my fate was decided. My name is Angel. So what does that mean? The biblical meaning would sound something like a spiritual being, supernatural; eternal spirit, Christ consciousness; a messenger of God. It's a name I would grow to hate, then ultimately love. Growing up with the name Angel, for some reason I was expected to be good, at least in the eyes of adults; I was expected to be perfect. Be in the world but not of the world. What exactly does that mean? I was five years old when this thought first occurred to me. I had this innate knowing that I was not from here, whatever that meant. I remember thinking, *Why am I here? What is the meaning of life? And what is God?* My family wasn't particularly religious. We had a few relics of religion around the house: a Bible on the coffee table, praying hands and a cross on the wall. My mom made sure we said our prayers before bed and grace before supper but other than that we didn't go to church. On my quest to know God, I asked my mom if I could go to church with a friend in my neighborhood. After talking to her grandmother, making sure it was safe, she allowed me to go. My first introduction to God was through the Pentecostal church of God in Christ. I was on my hero journey to find my direct personal experience with God, restore my spiritual gifts, and understand healing through faith. I quickly realized that in order to have deliverance I mustn't commit sin and I had to be perfect.

I was raised in the projects of Syracuse New York, born to an illiterate father and a traumatized mother. My father had a fourth-grade education; he couldn't read and write but he could build or fix anything. My mom was the only girl of nine brothers and was raised by an abusive stepfather. My mom had a sixth-grade education, slightly higher than my father, but for all intents and purposes, she was illiterate as well. My parents both worked really hard to provide for me and my older sister; we weren't necessarily on welfare, but we weren't far from it. They each carried their own childhood traumas and unhealed wounds. My home was a battleground of dysfunction and pain. My earliest memories are of being awakened to the screams of my mother, shattering glass, doors slamming and arguing in the middle of the night. As a young child I had no understanding of the ways in which my father not only physically and emotionally abused my mother but dishonored her as well. The cheating and physical abuse that my mother endured would last until my dad left her when I was eight years old. Due to the separation I wasn't able to go to church with my friend anymore. So I began reading the Bible and practicing the principles I learned in Sunday school and church. I had been baptized by the Holy Spirit, but I never quite made it to speaking in tongues.

What can I do? All is mine. The power of God lies within the word of God, the wisdom of God, the manifestation of God, and the will of God's intention to do the good work. I began to develop my own unique relationship with the divine through the seven gifts of the Holy Spirit: Knowledge, Wisdom, Understanding, Counsel, Fortitude, Piety, and Godliness. I attended Vacation Bible School during the summers and I began going to church with friends. This would afford me the opportunity to experience God in many different forms. I attended Kingdom Hall and studied Jehovah's Witness for a short time. I attended Catholic churches and Protestant churches of numerous denominations. I sought knowledge of all kinds as I began to study law, mathematics and science(s). In fifth and sixth grades I studied the origins of HIV and AIDS, which would become an area of divine service. My fifth-grade science project received honorable mention, my sixth-grade project earned a respectable third place. By the age of 12, I began to study numerology, astrology, and later tarot. By the age 14 I was introduced to the Nation of Gods and Earths, the Nation of Islam, and the practice of self-improvement, which would expand my religious studies into the beliefs, behaviors, and institutional per-spective of Islam, Judaism, Jainism, Hermeticism, Confucianism, Taoism, Hinduism, and Buddhism, seeking salvation and libera-tion from suffering. However, my suffering had only just begun.

Persecution would become a pattern in my existence. As a child I was expected to be perfect and do no wrong. I never really fit in with my peers and was often called a goody two-shoes. As I grew older things shifted and persecution took on another form, whereas I was considered evil and a bad influence. I was often blamed for things I didn't do, accused of lying when I was telling the truth, and not well-liked because there was just something about me. In high school I was frequently sent to in-school suspension for expressing my views, not standing for the pledge of allegiance, or doing my homework during class. My teachers refused to accept my homework because I didn't do it at home. I spent my lunch break in the library when the majority of my peers were socializing in the halls and cafeteria. I was kicked out of school for fighting, homeschooled, and couldn't graduate because I never completed my physical education requirements, so I dropped out.

I had my first encounter with intimate love; that left me heartbroken and in pain. The pain was nothing I ever experienced. I couldn't eat. I couldn't sleep. I had this gnawing pain that I just couldn't release. I was running a fever, so my mother took me to the emergency room. The doctor said I was lovesick. This was my first understanding of the mind-body connection and physical disease. He was my first, in what would become a series of emotional and physically abusive relationships, where I felt dishonored and unloved.

In an attempt to find myself I dibbled and dabbled in things that I am not proud of. I was introduced to my shadow, sin and the evils of man's creation. If it had not been for the mercy of God and through His unconditional love, I could have been murdered or imprisoned. I had strayed away from the divine and was living foul. I didn't even know myself. Worldly life hardened me. I couldn't show compassion; that was considered a sign of weakness. I had to be prepared to demand respect at all costs. After being disrespected, I ended up being incarcerated for felony assault which almost cost my career in another area of divine service. I was introduced to government, policy, institutional racism, and systemic injustice. I was fortunate to have studied law in my youth so I could navigate out of a system that has trapped hundreds of thousands of black and brown people. I was sentenced to a six-month conditional discharge.

I was an emotional and spiritual mess, and at the age of nineteen, I slipped into a deep depression and found myself in yet another abusive relationship and homeless. Through the chaos, I still knew that I had God's divine grace. Love is the manifestation of all creation, and the virtue of God's will, selflessness, and the benevolent concern for another; and God made me a mother. My son, to whose existence I owe my salvation, was born. The responsibility of being a mother was like a course in miracles. In order to be the best mother I could be and take good care of my son I had to change everything about my lifestyle. I stopped running the streets, got my GED, and started looking for work. I had applied for a job at the post office. I needed to type 45 words per minute. My typing skills were a bit rusty, but I really wanted the job. With little money I went to a thrift store and bought an old typewriter to practice on. I thought I was fully prepared, but I had no idea what was in store. The bus that I had boarded stopped short of the testing site and I had about 10 minutes to walk over two miles to the exam. I was running and stumbling, frantically trying to make it to the testing site. I made it, but my nerves were shot, and I was panicked. I passed the coding part of the exam, but I failed the typing portion by five words. Now I had to walk back two miles and wait an hour for the bus to come. I was heartbroken, but I didn't give up.

My mother allowed me to borrow money from my life insurance to buy my first vehicle. It had four colors and a leaking sunroof, but it got me and my son from point A to B. I found another job working in a factory and on my way home I was rear-ended, which left me out of work for two years. I had vowed to God that I would stay the course, so I decided to start my own astrology and tarot card reading business, a skill I kept hidden for many years. Mrs. Cleo was popular at the time, and I thought society was finally awakening to the fullest expression of creation. I applied for a government grant that would assist the disabled in becoming employable. The grant was for a business start-up loan of $15,000. Everyone told me that I would never be awarded a grant to open up a metaphysical business. But that didn't deter me. I did what I did best and went to the library and read everything I could find on the Internet about starting an online business, and how to write a business plan. I was awarded the grant and New Found Psychic Interpretations was born. The business did well for a few months but with the expansion of the Internet sales began to drop.

I began to question my faith and morals. A science I had practiced for ten years, I began to question if I was doing God's work or the devil's work? This would start my journey on a new path of higher spiritual awakening. I started studying the chakra system and energy healing. I started exploring my spiritual gifts with a daily practice of prayer, divine guidance, sitting in meditation awaiting divine instructions. I asked God who I was, and I heard God. I asked, "What am I?" and I heard, a divine spiritual being living a physical existence. I asked, "Where did I come from?" I heard, a long line of divine spiritual beings that have come before you. I asked, "Where I am going?" I heard, back to whence you came. I asked, "What is my spiritual connection?" I heard, divine love. I asked, "What is my foundation?" I heard, divine faith. I asked, "Dear God what is my purpose?" and I heard, to be of service. I was given the instruction to read Genesis chapter 1.

I was working as a typesetter, I lost my job, and my landlord, who would become my saving grace, put the house up for sale. I had to be out in 60 days. I was already two months behind in rent; I had no job and no money. I took a job selling life insurance. I had to travel to Albany for two weeks of unpaid training. While there I met a beautiful woman, to whom I am forever grateful. She had invited me to her home a few days earlier to have Thanksgiving dinner with her and her family. On the last morning of instruction, I packed up my van, checked out of my room and sat for the NYS Insurance exam. I passed the exam and was awarded a license to sell insurance. I got in my van to make the hour and a half drive back home and my van broke down. Destitute, with no money, I was stranded. I called home, and no one in my family could help me. God sent me an Angel. The woman who was so gracious just a few days prior welcomed me back into her home. Her partner took my van to his mechanic, paid for the repair, provided me with food and shelter, and I was able to make it home.

As soon as my taxes came, I sent her back the money she had so unselfishly given. I wanted to send more, but I had to pay my landlord back-rent and find a new place. I went to pay my landlord and she told me she would use my security deposit for one month rent and that I only had to pay for one month, and to use the money to find a new place to stay. I was so grateful. The insurance gig didn't work out. I was working on commissions and my soul just wouldn't allow me to take advantage of hard-working people. After struggling to find a job, I received another divine message. God said, go to nursing school. I enrolled and started school in January of 2002.

While enrolled in the nursing program I decided to dual-major in nursing and social work. I started to journal and write my future into existence. I applied for a CNA training class and was kicked out of the program for coming back to class two minutes late. My watch had gotten water in it and was running slow. I tried to explain it to my teacher but she didn't care. I had already been late one day because of the bus. The van that was fixed had been repossessed; I couldn't afford the payments. I applied for another CNA training course at another nursing home, and I worked nights on that job while going to school during the day. After the first few semesters in the nursing program, I tested out for my LPN. I got a job at another nursing home as an LPN. My nursing program found out that I was enrolled in another program when I had to have my advisor sign off for me to take 18 credits in the semester. I was told that I couldn't complete the nursing program and take another major and that I would never graduate with a dual degree, even though my GPA was a 3.7.

The next semester I failed one of my nursing exams, orthopedics, by one point. Ironically, I would later work on the orthopedic unit as an LPN and then RN for five years. My advisor, who was also the orthopedic nursing instructor, refused to let me retake the exam. I was discharged from the program, told that I couldn't reapply for six months; I couldn't take any other programs of study; and I had to retest on all the procedure skills I had already completed. I graduated that year with my Associate's in human services and the following year, my Applied Associate's in nursing. I would have to see this instructor every Thursday for years when she held clinical on the unit.

That same year, I was accused of falsifying a document for a new patient who was admitted late one evening to the nursing home I worked at. He had an order for fungal and hydrocortisone cream. Just the night before we had been told by the nursing supervisor that we couldn't sign and circle if a patient's medication was not available. We had to borrow from another patient and complete the treatment. He had HIV and no one wanted to go in his room. HIV didn't bother me; it was my life's work and passion. By this time, I was an HIV educator. I spent over an hour in his room, bathed him, performed oral care, and applied the creams to his wounds. The next day, an agency nurse that frequented the facility signed for his cream from the pharmacy and reported that I had signed for a treatment that I did not give. I was fired from my job. I had just purchased a brand-new car. The union said they would fight for me and later reneged.

I wasn't deterred. I had been through so much, and God had always seen me through. I got a job at Syracuse University as an HIV educator for adolescents in the African American community. Upstate Medical University is now my alma mater; I graduated with a minor in nursing education and a Master's in family psychiatry. I had no plans on applying for any jobs. I wanted to study for my exam and take a much-needed rest. While in community college I worked at a substance use treatment facility as an LPN; they were hiring a NP in Psychiatry. I had the chemical dependency experience. I had graduated a few years earlier with an associate degree in substance use. It seemed like everywhere I went someone was mentioning this job to me. I was so burnt out I just wanted to rest. God spoke and I applied for the job.

I was interviewed by three women. I had been recommended for the position. In my journal years earlier, I had written my academic plans, the GPA I wanted to achieve, and amount of money I intended to earn. The starting salary was the exact amount of money I had set my intentions on years earlier. John 15:18-19, ESV, *If the world hates you, know that it has hated me before it hated you. If you were of the world, the world would love you as its own; but because you are not of the world, but I chose you out of the world, therefore the world hates you.* What I've learned upon my journey of perseverance and faith is when I thought things were happening to me, they were happening for me and that I am never alone. I found God in every religion that I studied. I've seen God in every person I encountered. I've felt God in every breath that I take. I am a part of the ALL and the ALL is a part of me.

Dedication

To my son, to whose existence I owe my salvation. To my family, whose love and assistance is always given unselfishly and freely. To my day ones, on whose friendship and support I can always rely. And my soul tribe, whose presence along my journey has allowed me to achieve my fullest potential. I am so grateful!

 **Tamika Otis** is a self-proclaimed serial entrepreneur, equity warrior, and atmosphere shifter, Tamika's mission is to empower people to live their best lives. Among numerous enterprises she had a hand in forming, Tamika's most prized venture is her consulting firm. Tamika founded KABOD Consulting Group LLC in 2016 in response to a growing need for culturally competent grant writing services in her community. In 2020, KABOD relaunched as a full-service consulting agency that takes a holistic approach to business/organizational consultation and leadership/personal development.

Tamika is also Co-Founder of the Black Women Give Foundation based in Philadelphia, PA where the collective giving model is utilized to fund impactful grants to grass-roots non-profit organizations serving communities of color in Southeastern PA. Tamika believes in the power of storytelling in encouraging others to use their pain to create purpose, power, and peace. Her unique and relatable way of storytelling not only ushers in healing, but deliverance for all who have the opportunity to hear and learn from her story. Tamika is a sought-after subject matter expert and speaker around the areas of Entrepreneurship, Economic Development and Racial Equity. She is the proud Mom of two sons, Christian, 19 and Braylon, 12.

THROUGH THE MUD

Tamika Otis

"Shoot me...shoot me!" I screamed as the barrel of a Glock 19 was pointed at my temple. The person holding the gun was my boyfriend, someone I had loved since I was 14. Here I was barely 21 years of age and in that moment the thought of being without him was worse than my own death.

Earlier that night he and I were having a seemingly normal and fun evening. We were watching movies and enjoying some libations, as we often did. I got up to use the bathroom and left my cell phone on the table. I thought nothing of it because I had nothing to hide. While I was in the bathroom, I could hear my boyfriend arguing. That wasn't uncommon. He was a drug dealer, a 6'6" football stature of a man that no one ever wanted to mess with. When I returned to the living room, he looked at me with the coldest look in his eyes, absent of any love. I asked what was wrong and he began packing up my things and telling me to get out. I kept asking why and trying to take my things out of his hands. He said a guy called my phone and he answered. This person proceeded to tell him that I had been in a hotel with him the night before. It wasn't true. I didn't even know this person. I tried everything to reason with my boyfriend. In desperation I screamed out my alibis to prove I couldn't have been where this person said I was the night before. I tried to caress his face, tell him to look in my eyes. "I would never do that to you," I exclaimed. But nothing I said mattered. He believed what was said and felt disrespected and betrayed. In his mind, I had to go.

He kept trying to push me and my bags toward the door. I dropped to my knees in an effort to stop him from getting me there. He began to drag me by my feet, screaming for me to "get the (expletive) out of my house or I'll kill you." I was relentless in my effort to stay. He couldn't get me out. I used all the strength inside me to push my legs up against the front door so he wouldn't open it. Finally, it seemed like he had given up. I sat in a ball at the front door with my knees to my chest, partly relieved that I was able to get him to "allow" me to stay and partly petrified at the fury in his eyes like I had never seen before. It seemed as soon as he walked away, he was back, grabbing my now nearly limp body and dragging me into the kitchen. He propped me up on the counter, grabbed my hair by balling the back of it, and slowly put a gun right to my head. "I said get the (expletive) out of my house or I will kill you," he said with a calm rage that gave me chills throughout my body. "Shoot me then, because I'm not leaving," was my response. And I kept saying it as if no other words could come from my mouth. He was biting his bottom lip and gritting his teeth while pushing the gun harder and harder into my head. I'd love to say I knew he wasn't going to shoot me but the truth is, I had absolutely no idea what he was capable of. "Please just shoot me," I begged him. He finally shook his head, called me a "crazy bitch," walked into his bedroom and closed the door. And I…followed him.

Looking back, that was the most defining moment in recognizing I did not value myself. For whatever reason, I always attached my worth to other people, mostly men. If they didn't want me, I must not be worthy of their love. If they mistreated me, I must have done something to deserve it. Or even more, I had to do the extraordinary to prove my love. As much as me telling my then boyfriend to "shoot me" was about not wanting to leave, it was also my dysfunctional way of proving my worth. *You matter so much that the thought of being without you is worse than death.*

This was sadly only one in a series of dysfunctional and abusive relationships. It was a pattern that perpetuated because I did not know or embrace my worth. And this lack of self-honor and self-love caused me to make horrible decisions that would cause pain, fear and disappointment to become a common theme in my life.

I was trying every way but God's way in determining my worth. I masked the tremendous pain and unresolved trauma that rested on my heart by using drugs, drinking heavily, having promiscuous sex, and all I felt was empty. Then God allowed me to hit rock bottom. I could no longer run away from the painful memories of being mistreated. I could no longer continue to choose to dishonor myself. To get my undivided attention, God allowed me to enter into a time of isolation, which is an unwanted yet necessary part of everyone's healing journey.

In my time of isolation, God not only showed me what life could be if I surrendered to His will but also showed me how resilient I already was. Despite how low I felt, the truth was, I had already emerged from some situations that others didn't. He kept a whisper in my heart no matter how far from Him I thought I was. He kept reminding me of all He had already done to preserve my life and all He could do if I allowed Him. So I was determined to turn my pain into purpose and even more than that...into peace. I became intent on letting resilience be my history teacher.

Do you know that you are resilient? Do you tap into it when the days are hard? Do you remember what you've been through? Because like many women living the Black experience in America, you've been THROUGH a lot. Through by definition means "moving in one side and out of the other side or continuing in time toward completion of a process or period." So when you say you're "going through it," you are actually affirming that you are going to come out of it on the other side. That's the resilience in you speaking, the voice that no matter how much it's stifled, reminds you that this too shall pass—that you have the power inside you to shift any circumstance and the lessons learned will position you for better in the future. Resilience…it's such a beautiful gift.

Resilient means "able to withstand or recover quickly from difficult conditions; able to recoil or spring back into shape after bending, stretching or being compressed." Resilience is toughness and the ability to bounce back. It helps you to propel and not just move forward. No matter how much you've been stretched or bent, no matter how suffocating life feels at times, resilience says you have the ability to withstand AND recover. Are you being intentional about tapping into the resilience inside you?

During one of my speaking engagements, I broke down the letters in the word **RESILIENT** to create a blueprint of sorts. Let's look at these letters and use them to help us better understand how we can awaken or strengthen the resilience inside us.

The first letter in the word resilient is 'R.' This reminds me of the need to *REGROUP*. Regroup means "to become reorganized in order to make a fresh start," or even deeper, when speaking in terms of the military, it means "to become organized in a new tactical formation."

Isn't it when life seems so out of control that we have to "regroup?" Life tends to get into a state of chaos and disorganization. Do you find yourself often saying, "I don't even know where to start?" or "This is too much?" That's your cue to regroup. Start reordering and reorganizing the areas of your life that you have influence over. Don't forsake the little things. Like your morning routine. Your prayer closet. Your exercise schedule. Meditation.

Sleep. Whatever it is that helps you to recenter, take a deep breath and plot your strategy.

There is a song I love to listen to when I'm in process. It's called *"ENCOURAGE Yourself."* Often, when we find ourselves having to regroup, we also find ourselves in a state of isolation. Whether real or perceived, it feels as though we are all alone or that the people who would usually be our source of encouragement are eerily silent. Do you know that nothing is happening to you, and everything is happening for you? Even that season of isolation. As mentioned earlier, isolation is a necessary and critical component of your healing. Your distractions are removed and you enter into this beautiful fellowship of only you and GOD.

This is where you *SPEAK* life into your situation as you continue the act of regrouping. Don't underestimate the power behind encouraging yourself. Remind yourself of who and WHOSE you are every day, or every hour if needed. Speak into the atmosphere. Also, mind your words. Death and life are in the power of the tongue. Be mindful of the words that you allow into the atmosphere. You can change your world by changing your words. Also, change the things you see around you. I had a custom piece made that I put in my bedroom. It's a very simple piece that says, *"Ease Calm Flow is my natural state."* That is the first thing I see when I open my eyes in the morning. And I whisper it to myself before I begin my day. How do you encourage yourself and speak life over your situation?

A big part of being resilient is being **INTENTIONAL** in everything you do. Because it all matters. It's often when we become so unintentional in our living and interactions that our life becomes unbalanced and chaotic. Are you setting your intentions every morning? Are you being intentional about creating a life that is peaceful, not just powerful? What about being intentional about creating an atmosphere that nurtures and cultivates your healing?

You can't get healed in the same environment you got sick in... notice I didn't say the same *place* you got sick in. See, you can shift the environment and atmosphere of a place. Are you a thermostat or a thermometer? Thermometers adjust to the temperature. If it's cold in a room it shows that it's cold, same for if it's hot. It allows the climate to dictate its response. But a thermostat sets and regulates the climate in the room. When it gets too hot, it's programmed to cool the room down and vice versa. Ask yourself, are you a thermostat or thermometer? Are you regulating the climate around you or are you assimilating or adjusting to it? Are you intentional?

The next letter in resilient is 'L' for LIMIT. I'm sure you think I'm going to say "the sky is the limit" here, don't you? NOPE. Here is where I tell you to limit your interactions with negative people, places and things. Limit the negative self-talk. Limit the things you use to get through the day. Can I be honest? There was a period of time that I was going through three or four bottles of tequila by myself in a week. I wanted to buffer my pain. Limit your buffers. Allow yourself to feel. Allow your heart to break. Allow your anger and shame to come off you. But limit the time you stay in that space. You can put your foot on the brake for a moment, just don't shift the gear into park. What are some of the things you are going to limit or eliminate to help manifest the resilience inside of you?

Once you limit distractions, buffers and any and everything that would cause you to impede or sabotage your healing, the next thing I encourage you to do is to enter into a time of *INTROSPECTION*.

The definition of introspection is "self-examination, analyzing yourself, looking at your own personality and actions, and considering your own motivations." An example of introspection is when you meditate to try to understand your feelings. Time spent alone in thought can be positive—you can create an environment for personal growth and creativity—but it can also be dangerous when we are negatively turned against ourselves. That's why it's so important for this step to happen after you have regrouped, encouraged yourself, spoken life into your situation and limited the things that hinder you from manifesting your heart's desires. It's only through the process of introspection that we identify what our intentions are and lean on God for direction. Your introspection is a necessary component of your isolation, which is a necessary component of your healing. Don't try and skip that part. Get very clear on who you are but ground that clarity in first knowing WHOSE you are.

Next, EMPOWER yourself. This is a trendy word now but it's important to know its true definition: "Give (someone) the authority or power to do something; make (someone) stronger and more confident, especially in controlling their life and claiming their rights." So often we look to outside sources to empower or encourage us. But just like encouraging yourself, you can empower yourself too. You can take everything you're reading right now—your regrouping, encouraging yourself, speaking life into your situation, being intentional about how you move on a day-to-day basis, limiting negative people, things and habits and going into a period of introspection—and EMPOWER yourself to create the life you love. It's all already inside you. Why are you looking for what is already inside you? Do you not remember what you have been through? Do you not know that your latter days SHALL be greater than your former days? And that sense of empowerment you create emanates into the atmosphere and gives permission for everyone around you to do the same for themselves.

And now it is time to NURTURE or "care for and encourage the growth or development of" yourself. When you create this new safe, peaceful and powerful space inside you, you have to nurture it. Care for it. Give it the right conditions to grow. When the weeds start to pop up, pull them. When the pests of doubt and worry come, get rid of them. Love on yourself. War for yourself. Remember your five-year-old self, or the you before the world and the conditions in it changed your worldview. Let her know you got this, and everything is going to be okay. On the days you feel too weak to fight for yourself, fight for the little girl in you. Nurture her and in doing so you will usher in the healing you need right now. How will you nurture yourself going forward?

And finally, the last letter in resilient is 'T'. Be ye TRANSFORMED by the renewing of your mind. To transform something or someone means "to change them completely and suddenly." Your resilience transforms you. It reawakens you. Suddenly. When you surrender completely to the will of God, the transformation that takes place in your life is swift. Resilience confirms and affirms all the greatness that is inside you. Allow resilience to walk you to the door of transformation.

Being resilient does not mean that everything around you will suddenly be all good all the time. In fact, much like the Bible tells us that God's strength is perfected in our weakness (II Corinthians 12:9), your resilience is perfected through the hard times. Today's world can feel so overwhelming. Our once optimistic outlooks on life have too often been exchanged for the expectation that things will only get worse or that the light will never shine again. When there is so much uncertainty and things are so unbelievably out of our control, it's a natural human emotion to shut down.

I was talking to a friend the other day who shared how heavy and restless she was feeling. She said, "I could always at least see the light at the end of the tunnel even if it looked so far away, but now it's just dark. I can't even see the light." I silently agreed with her but at the same moment I had a vision of a tunnel that had a winding road. I closed my eyes and envisioned myself driving in a tunnel and going around bends. After about the third bend, I could again see the light. That instantly changed my perspective.

When in the midst of trouble, we frequently forget that this life is full of twists and turns. However, the twists and turns of life do not invalidate the truth that the sun shines every morning, no matter how dark the night. It doesn't matter that we cannot see or feel the sun when it makes way for the light of the moon. We have audacious confidence that when we awake the sun will shine again. And just like the tunnel, when you stay the course of the winding road you will again see the light.

Even more, God gave us a beautiful and tangible example of the resilience we each have inside of us. When I reflect on the lotus flower, one of the most beautiful and unique flowers on the planet, I remember that even though it emerges from the mud, once it blooms and breaks the surface of the water, the lotus flower is entirely unmarked by the dirt that surrounded it. Just like the lotus flower, we too have the ability to rise from the mud, bloom out of the darkness and radiate into the world.

Don't reflect on where you are right now, because even in the mud, through sheer determination, resilience and faith, you too can emerge unscathed. Start from where you are. Believe you can shift the atmosphere. Your healing is wrapped up in your action. Follow the blueprint. Move in faith, knowing everything you need is already inside you. And surely, just like the lotus flower, you too can make it through the mud, without a trace of what you've been through.

Dedication

This chapter is dedicated to every sister who lost her voice. To every woman who has been shamed rather than empowered by their past experience. To every woman who feels all alone and is yearning for some fellowship with other women who can amplify her voice. This is for every woman who allowed others besides GOD to determine their worth and value. This chapter is for every woman that is on the cusp of their breakthrough and just needed to hear that they are not alone and that everything needed to manifest their breakthrough is already inside them. You are worthy. You are strong. You are capable. You are RESILIENT. Stand in it, sis! God bless you.

ABOUT THE VISIONARY AUTHOR

ArDenay Garner is a personal development trainer, executive producer of the Me, Myself & God Tours, Inc., founder of Develop Your Purpose Academy, owner of ArDenay Innerprize LLC., and best-selling author of Divine Invitations. ArDenay provides coaching, speaking, and consulting services for visionary leaders and entrepreneurs who want to write and publish their personal story to promote compassion and world healing. She has hosted numerous events including her signature LOVE Campaigns, award ceremonies, and various seminars and workshops helping over 300 women reclaim their self-confidence.

ArDenay's new mission is to help 79,000 women develop their purpose through writing their personal story of perseverance, faith, survivorship, recovery, reconciliation, leadership, and entrepreneurship, to promote compassion and world healing. When she is not traveling or spending quality time with her loving husband and children, in Upstate New York, you can find ArDenay having candid conversations in her Divine Invitations Club on Clubhouse.